SOCIAL WORKERS

PRACTICAL CAREER GUIDES
Series Editor: Kezia Endsley

Clean Energy Technicians, by Marcia Santore
Computer Game Development & Animation, by Tracy Brown Hamilton
Craft Artists, by Marcia Santore
Criminal Justice Professionals, by Kezia Endsley
Culinary Arts, by Tracy Brown Hamilton
Dental Assistants and Hygienists, by Kezia Endsley
Digital Communications Professionals, by Kezia Endsley
Education Professionals, by Kezia Endsley
Electricians, by Marcia Santore
Financial Managers, by Marcia Santore
Fine Artists, by Marcia Santore
First Responders, by Kezia Endsley
Ground Transportation Professionals, by Marcia Santore
Health and Fitness Professionals, by Kezia Endsley
Information Technology (IT) Professionals, by Erik Dafforn
Marketing Professionals, by Kezia Endsley
Mathematicians and Statisticians, by Kezia Endsley
Media and Journalism Professionals, by Tracy Brown Hamilton
Medical Office Professionals, by Marcia Santore
Multimedia and Graphic Designers, by Kezia Endsley
Nursing Professionals, by Kezia Endsley
Plumbers, by Marcia Santore
Skilled Trade Professionals, by Corbin Collins
Social Workers, by Tracy Brown Hamilton
Substance Abuse Counselors, by Tracy Brown Hamilton
Veterinarian Technicians and Assistants, by Kezia Endsley
Writers and Authors, by Tracy Brown Hamilton

SOCIAL WORKERS
A Practical Career Guide

TRACY BROWN HAMILTON

ROWMAN & LITTLEFIELD
Lanham • Boulder • New York • London

Published by Rowman & Littlefield
An imprint of The Rowman & Littlefield Publishing Group, Inc.
4501 Forbes Boulevard, Suite 200, Lanham, Maryland 20706
www.rowman.com

86-90 Paul Street, London EC2A 4NE, United Kingdom

Copyright © 2022 by The Rowman & Littlefield Publishing Group, Inc.

All rights reserved. No part of this book may be reproduced in any form or by any electronic or mechanical means, including information storage and retrieval systems, without written permission from the publisher, except by a reviewer who may quote passages in a review.

British Library Cataloguing in Publication Information Available

Library of Congress Cataloging-in-Publication Data
Names: Hamilton, Tracy Brown, author.
Title: Social workers : a practical career guide / Tracy Brown Hamilton.
Description: Lanham : Rowman & Littlefield Publishing Group, [2022] | Series: Practical career guides | Includes bibliographical references. | Summary: "Social Workers: A Practical Career Guide, which includes interviews with professionals in this field which has proven to be a stable, lucrative, and growing profession"—Provided by publisher.
Identifiers: LCCN 2021034078 (print) | LCCN 2021034079 (ebook) | ISBN 9781538159248 (paperback) | ISBN 9781538159255 (epub)
Subjects: LCSH: Social workers. | Career development. | Social Service—Vocational guidance.
Classification: LCC HV41 .H286 2022 (print) | LCC HV41 (ebook) | DDC 361—dc23
LC record available at https://lccn.loc.gov/2021034078
LC ebook record available at https://lccn.loc.gov/2021034079

Contents

Introduction   vii

1   Why Choose a Career as a Social Worker?   1
2   Forming a Career Plan   19
3   Pursuing the Education Path   39
4   Writing Your Résumé and Interviewing   59

Notes   73
Glossary   77
Further Resources   81
Bibliography   83
About the Author   85

Introduction

So You Want a Career as a Social Worker

Congratulations! By picking up this book, you have taken an important step toward deciding whether a career in social work is right for you. This likely means you are interested in helping people to overcome difficulties, be they financial, legal, interpersonal, or related to abuse or addiction.

Perhaps you or someone you know has turned to a social worker for assistance with a tough situation in the past. Regardless of your reasons, reading this book is a positive first step in understanding the role of a social worker, what a social worker does and the various places social workers do their jobs, what kind of education and experience the field requires, and, most importantly, whether this is the right career choice for you.

A career such as one in social work, which allows you to have a direct, positive impact on people and the communities in which they live, is definitely satisfying. Because of the nature of the work—helping to improve situations for clients you represent—the job also involves coming face-to-face with less-than-ideal circumstances, which can be difficult to deal with day in, day out.

To do the job of a social worker effectively and at minimal risk of burnout to yourself, being strong in the following skills and characteristics is enormously beneficial (if you are naturally strong in these areas, then you are off to a great start!):

- **Communication skills:** A social worker depends heavily on his or her communication skills. Working with clients to help them face challenges requires open and trusting communication, so you, as the social worker, fully understand the situation your client is in. Social workers have to be very good not only at communicating their counsel and advice but at listening and understanding their clients' needs in order to arrive at an effective strategy to help them.

- **Emotional skills:** Most people who seek out or require the services of a social worker are doing so because they are in a stressful, challenging situation. It is important as a social worker to listen not just closely but with empathy, patience, and compassion and to not express any judgment.
- **Interpersonal skills:** "Interpersonal" skills are also called people skills or soft skills. They refer to strengths that help with relating to other people. Social workers need to be strong with these skills in order to work well with different groups of people and to form good relationships with clients and colleagues.
- **Organizational skills:** Organizational skills will be an asset in any line of work naturally, but in the field of social work, they are especially important. Although face-to-face contact with clients can be a large part of the job, another large part is all the paperwork that comes with the cases you manage as a social worker. Keeping track of clients and their treatment plans or other strategies related to improving their situation is essential and requires a lot of organization.
- **Problem-solving skills:** The entire function of social work is to improve circumstances and find solutions where things are not working well. Being a creative and intelligent problem solver is a major part of the job. Social workers need to develop practical and innovative solutions to their clients' problems in order to succeed.

This book is the ideal start for understanding the role of a social worker, the various environments in which social workers work, and what path you should follow to ensure you have all the training, education, and experience needed to succeed in your future career goals. It will help you understand how to begin now, whether you are a middle school or high school student or a university graduate, to set yourself on the course to a successful career as a social worker.

A Career as a Social Worker

According to *Merriam-Webster*, a social worker performs "any of various professional activities or methods concretely concerned with providing social services and especially with the investigation, treatment, and material aid of the economically, physically, mentally, or socially disadvantaged."[1] This is a bit of a mouthful, but that's because the term "social work" does encompass a lot of activities and functions, which will be discussed throughout this book.

In essence, a social worker does any of the following:

- supports people and communities in need of help;
- assesses the needs of clients, including their existing situations and circumstances and what is working in their favor (strengths, support networks) and what hurdles they are facing, to determine their goals;
- helps clients come to terms with and adjust to changes and challenges they are facing, such as illness, divorce, abuse, addiction, or unemployment;
- researches, refers, and advocates for community resources, such as food stamps, child care, and health care, to assist and improve a client's well-being;
- responds to crisis situations such as child abuse and mental health emergencies to ensure the safety of clients or the party for whom they are advocating (such as children);
- continues to follow up with clients once an action plan is in place to ensure plans are being adhered to and situations are improving;
- maintains case files and records;
- develops and evaluates programs and services to ensure that basic client needs are met; and
- in some cases provides therapy.

Note: The ongoing coronavirus pandemic has seen a rise in substance abuse problems, as people struggle with the isolation of lockdowns and working or studying from home.[2] Loneliness, isolation, fear, and in some cases the loss of loved ones have put many at risk for mental health issues and abuse, such as domestic violence. Many people have also faced new financial difficulty due to job loss.

At the same time, because of social-distancing precautions, many people have not been able to seek out inpatient counseling in the traditional way. Social workers have also had to adjust how they work with clients, with many having to adapt to online, virtual counseling sessions. As vaccinations become more widely available, it is hoped that the lockdown will come to an end, but the effects the pandemic has had on people's lives may be felt for a longer period.

Social workers hold degrees in social work or a related field such as psychology or sociology, all of which will be discussed later in the book. Some jobs in social work require a master's degree—an advanced college degree that typically takes two years to earn, which we will cover in a later chapter—but for other jobs a bachelor's degree is sufficient. In any case, you can expect to be required to hold a college degree in order to have a successful career in social work.

The Market Today

How does the job market look for young people seeking to work in the social work field? It's actually a very fast-growing field, making it a smart career choice.

> "When you are working with someone, trying to get them unstuck, over the speed bump they're faced with on their life's journey, and something clicks for them, that feels like magic. Helping people understand how and why they have emotions, and what the heck to do with them when they are there, is incredibly satisfying."
> —Michelle Hominick Anderson, registered social worker and addiction counselor

According to the US Bureau of Labor Statistics, employment for social workers in the United States is projected to grow a strong 13 percent between 2019 and 2029.[3] This is a far greater rate of growth than average for an occupation. This is a positive projection, both for those in the social worker profession and for those seeking the support of a social worker.

What Does This Book Cover?

This book covers the following topics relating to social work–related careers:

- understanding what social workers do and what characteristics many who land in these fields possess;
- how to form a career plan—starting now, wherever you are in your education—and how to start taking the steps that will best lead to success;
- educational requirements and opportunities and how to fulfill them;

INTRODUCTION

Becoming a social worker gives you the opportunity to have a positive and direct impact on the lives, health, well-being, and relationships of people and communities struggling with a variety of challenges. *Hiraman/E+/Getty Images.*

- tips on writing your résumé, interviewing, networking, and applying for jobs; and
- resources for further information.

Where Do You Start?

As this book will show, no matter where you are in your education, from junior high to college graduate and beyond, it is never too soon to get started pursuing a career in social work. Whether you are reading up on the latest practices of social workers and the particular clientele they serve, keeping abreast of societal issues that require social workers to manage or resolve, or brushing up on related skills in classes offered by your college or high school, you can start your career preparation now.

Once you've read this book, you will be well on your way to understanding what kind of career you want, what you can expect from it, and how to go about planning and beginning your path. Let's get started.

1

Why Choose a Career as a Social Worker?

Are you interested in a career that allows you the opportunity to gain a deeper understanding of the challenges people and communities face and to have a part in solving them? Are you a good listener and reliable confidant? Are you nonjudgmental with a genuine interest in helping people overcome their struggles and live happier, healthier lives with the resources they need to support them?

Are you interested in how social systems work and in community in general? Do you care about social issues, such as education, employment, substance abuse, and the like? Having a career as a social worker means being in a position to help people and communities achieve safety and well-being. It is a challenging and rewarding field to pursue.

Choosing a career is a difficult task, but as we discuss in more detail in chapter 2, there are many methods and means of support to help you refine your career goal and hone in on a profession that will be satisfying and will fit you and your natural characteristics and interests the best.

Of course, the first step is understanding what a particular field—in this case social work—actually encompasses and informing yourself about the future outlook of the profession. That is the emphasis of this chapter, which looks at defining the field in general and then more specific terms, as well as examining the past and predicted future of the field.

As with any career, there are pros and cons. In balancing the good points and less attractive points of a career, you must ask yourself whether, in the end, the positive outweighs any negatives you may discover. This chapter will also help you decide whether a career in social work is actually the right choice for you. And if you decide it is, the next chapter will offer further suggestions for how to prepare your career path, including questions to ask yourself and resources to help you determine more specifically what kind of career related to social work suits you the very best.

What Are the Different Career Paths You Can Pursue as a Social Worker?

As mentioned in the introduction, social workers perform their jobs in various environments. You find social workers in schools, in treatment facilities, in prisons, in private practices, and in hospitals, for example. Social workers also work with various groups of people or types of clientele, which can include individuals or families facing different difficulties for different reasons. The types of services required vary with each case.

Although there are a number of "types" of social worker—it is a broad field, so you have many avenues and specialties of focus to choose from—this book will primarily focus on the following:

- child and family social workers,
- school social workers,
- health-care social workers, and
- mental health and substance abuse social workers.

The following explains in more detail some of the specific types of social workers that exist and the types of problems they work to solve and clients with whom they work.

CHILD WELFARE SOCIAL WORKERS

Child welfare social workers work to solve conflicts and problems that arise in families and households with young children. This type of social worker serves as an advocate for children, meaning it is their priority and central role to represent and "speak" for the child or children and to ensure that the needs of the child or children are met and that the environment in which they live is a safe and loving one. The child social worker is there to help the child and to protect them from any harm caused by abuse or neglect.

CLINICAL SOCIAL WORKERS

Clinical social workers are focused on providing therapy to individuals and families suffering from any number of mental health issues, such as depression. Licensed clinical social workers (LCSWs) are permitted in some states to diagnose and treat mental health disorders, including depression and anxiety. They often work in private practices, hospitals, or neighborhood mental health agencies.

FORENSIC SOCIAL WORKERS (CRIMINAL JUSTICE)

Forensic social workers apply established principles of social work to questions and issues relating to legal matters and litigation, both criminal and civil. Some cases in which forensic social workers may be involved include corrections, child custody, and juvenile services.

GERONTOLOGICAL SOCIAL WORKERS

As part of the system of health-care social work, gerontological social workers help older (geriatric) clients and their families with locating services such as home health care and meal delivery. This type of social worker can further assist older adults as they transition into a nursing care or assisted living facility.

HOSPICE AND PALLIATIVE SOCIAL WORKERS

The classification of hospice and palliative social workers falls within the category of health-care social work. Their responsibility is to help patients and their families cope with a terminal illness. Hospice and palliative social workers provide grief counseling or connect patients and their loved ones to outside resources that may include support groups.

MEDICAL SOCIAL WORKERS

Medical social workers are another branch of social workers within the health-care social work structure. They help patients cope with chronic or terminal illnesses through psychological and social support. Other duties include discharge planning, assisting patients in connecting with other services, organizing support groups, and performing home visits to recently discharged patients.

MILITARY SOCIAL WORKERS

Military social workers provide military members and their families with resources they need to succeed in areas such as mental health and employment. Other social work opportunities within the military vary and include clinical work at Veterans Affairs hospitals.

PEDIATRIC SOCIAL WORKERS

Pediatric social workers join physicians to provide a holistic approach to children and their families faced with medical adversity. While it is typical for a sick child to be the primary client, pediatric social workers may provide support to a child with a parent or family member suffering a health condition.

PSYCHIATRIC (MENTAL HEALTH) SOCIAL WORKERS

Psychiatric social work is a type of medical social work that involves supporting, providing therapy to, and coordinating the care of people with severe mental illness who require hospitalization or other types of intensive psychiatric help.

PRIVATE PRACTICE SOCIAL WORKERS

Depending on state regulations, private practice social workers may offer clinical and nonclinical services. Clinical work may involve counseling and providing psychotherapy to individuals, couples, families, and groups. Nonclinical services may include mediation, education, and conflict resolution, among others.

SCHOOL SOCIAL WORKERS

These professionals work with children at every grade level. The responsibilities of school social workers include assisting students with issues, such as truancy and behavior, that can affect academic progress. As an advocate for children, school social workers connect with outside agencies and resources when necessary.

MACRO SOCIAL WORKERS

Macro social workers focus on fostering positive change in a community based on the diversity and cultural values of its residents. They join community leaders and residents to develop solutions that help resolve issues, encourage involvement, and improve the community.

SUBSTANCE ABUSE SOCIAL WORKERS

A substance abuse social worker is a specific type of social worker who assesses and treats people and families of people who are suffering from substance abuse problems. This can include addictions to alcohol and illegal or prescription drugs.

A BRIEF HISTORY OF THE SOCIAL WORK PROFESSION[1]

In the late nineteenth century, a strange paradox was observed in the United States and Europe: despite a strengthening economy, poverty was increasing. This was the root of social work as a cause and a service. It was originally intended as a volunteer effort to help this so-called social question but became an actual job by 1900.

As early as 1920, social workers could be found working in places such as public schools and hospitals, as well as child welfare agencies. Most of the work was focused on helping children and families with children.

As time went on, a more formal social work method was established and social work education programs were expanded. Social work achieved professional status by the 1930s.

Social workers are often associated with addressing issues relating to poverty, which in fact was initially the focus of social work, but this increasingly extended to concern for the well-being of families and children in particular beginning in the 1920s.

Social work evolved again when crises such as the Great Depression and World War II brought to light mental health concerns, which became the focus of programs for veterans and the general public that provided in- and outpatient mental health services. By the twenty-first century, social work was licensed in all fifty states.

Social work celebrated its centennial in 1998. This date commemorated one hundred years of professional social work, celebrating the first classes in social work, which were offered at Columbia University in New York in the summer of 1898.

Social workers serve individuals and communities by being a resource to help provide access to services like health care, financial support, education, protection from violence, or safe living conditions—among others. *sturti/E+/Getty Images.*

The Pros and Cons of a Career in Social Work

As with any career, one in social work carries with it upsides and downsides. But also true is that one person's "pro" is another person's "con." If you consider yourself a strong interpersonal communicator and an attentive listener, you will likely thrive in in-person counseling sessions with groups or individuals. If you seek a reliably nine-to-five life with a predictable schedule, you may struggle with the long hours and tendency for social workers to bring work home with them, if only mentally. There are lots of aspects to consider when choosing the right career for you.

Although there is a lot of variety within the social work field (as far as in what environment you work and with what clientele or specialization focus),

Tip: Although it's one thing to read about the pros and cons of a particular career, the best way to really get a feel for what a typical day is like on the job and what the challenges and rewards are is to talk to someone who is already working in the profession or who has in the past.

- **Am I a trustworthy confidant? Am I able to keep secrets and preserve the confidentiality others entrust in me?**
  As a social worker, your success will depend on clients being able to freely and confidently open up to you, to share feelings and experiences they may never have openly discussed with another person.
- **Am I naturally inquisitive, and do I know how to ask the right questions to lead to deeper understanding of an issue?**
  A natural curiosity and attentiveness to the social issues that affect people and communities—local, national, or global—are essential as a social worker. Do you care about what is going on around you? Are you interested in understanding why things are as they are and how they can be improved?
- **Am I tolerant and nonjudgmental?**
  Social workers have a responsibility to be unbiased and ethical. This means not taking sides or reacting emotionally but following the law and being fair when making recommendations or decisions in your work.
- **Can I consistently deal with people in a professional, friendly way?**
  Communication is key to success in the social worker field. Your interpersonal communication skills need to be exceptional when interacting with clients and their families or with other officials and experts involved in a particular case in order to have effective and open discussions about the issues at hand and the approach to actions being taken.
- **Do I have an overly excited attention to detail and an inability to leave any stone unturned?**
  Do you give up easily or do you have the fortitude to keep probing, keep thinking, keep searching for new answers and approaches? Most problems are not resolved overnight. A social worker needs to be able to commit to a long-term relationship in some cases in order to help someone through their challenges.
- **Can I function under pressure without risking my own well-being?**
  Social work is not the kind of profession that enables you to shut down your computer at 5 p.m. and go home and think about something else until the next morning. Social workers are vulnerable to taking their work home with them and to being available at all hours. To avoid burnout, it is important to have strategies to deal with this kind of pressure as well as the emotional drain of thinking deeply about other people's struggles.

> ## WHERE DO SOCIAL WORKERS EARN THE MOST?
>
> Social work is sometimes associated with lower-than-average earnings, which is an inaccurate impression. We've already looked at median income statistics for social work careers earlier in this chapter, but how much a social worker can earn annually also varies from state to state (and, of course, from province to province or county to county—all depending on where you live and practice).
>
> So in which US states are social workers earning the highest salaries? According to data gathered by socialwork.org, here are the states where social workers are earning the most and their average pay.[3] Note this information is based on combining data from the BLS for the average salaries for four different types of social workers, including child, family, and school; health care; mental health and substance abuse; and all other "types" of social workers.
>
> - California: $68,910
> - Connecticut: $68,000
> - Nevada: $64,890
> - New Hampshire: $62,300
> - Maine: $61,140
> - New Jersey: $68,380
> - District of Columbia: $65,950
> - Hawaii: $63,200
> - Maryland: $62,140
> - New York: $60,700

One way to see if you may be cut out for a career in social work is to ask yourself the following questions:

- **Do I genuinely care about other people?**
  The central role of a social worker of any "type" is to help another person overcome a difficulty that is having a negative impact on their lives—to understand and resolve issues that are affecting their well-being. Although most people will say that, yes, they care about others, that is not the same as dedicating your career to making other people's lives better.

Thinking about what kind of career suits you the best can feel frustrating and intimidating because it requires you to ask yourself important questions that only you can answer. There are, however, many sources online that can direct you to understand what characteristics a particular job, such as social work, relies on the most to help you decide if it's a good fit. *GlobalStock/E+/Getty Images.*

For now, let's look at the general demands and responsibilities of a career in social work—as mentioned previously in the section on pros and cons—and suggest some questions that may help you discover whether such a profession is a good match for your personality, interests, and the general lifestyle you want to keep in the future.

Although there is not one "type" that matches the profile of a successful social worker, you can anticipate some aspects of the job and think about whether you would naturally enjoy them or expect to struggle with them.

Note: Of course, no job is going to match every aspect of your personality or fit your every desire, especially when you are just starting out. There are, however, some aspects to a job that may be so unappealing or simply mismatched that you may decide to opt for something else, or equally you may be so drawn to a feature of a job that any downsides are not that important.

WHAT IS A MEDIAN INCOME?

Throughout your job search, you might hear the term "median income" used. What does it mean? Some people believe it's the same thing as "average income," but that's not correct. While the median income and average income might sometimes be similar, they are calculated in different ways.

The true definition of median income is the income at which half of the workers earn more than that income and the other half of workers earn less. If this is complicated, think of it this way: Suppose there are five employees in a company, each with varying skills and experience. Here are their salaries:

- $42,500
- $48,250
- $51,600
- $63,120
- $86,325

What is the median income? In this case, the median income is $51,600, because of the five total positions listed, it is in the middle. Two salaries are higher than $51,600, and two are lower.

The "average income" is simply the total of all salaries divided by the number of total jobs. In this case, the average income is $58,359.

Why does this matter? The median income is a more accurate way to measure the various incomes in a set because it's less likely to be influenced by extremely high or low numbers in the total group of salaries. In our example of five incomes, the highest income ($86,325) is much higher than the other incomes, and therefore it makes the average income ($58,359) higher than most incomes in the group. Therefore, if you base your income expectations on the average, you'll likely be disappointed to eventually learn that most incomes are below it.

But if you look at median income, you'll always know that half the people are above it and half are below it. That way, depending on your level of experience and training, you'll have a better estimate of where you'll end up on the salary spectrum.

How Healthy Is the Job Market for Social Workers?

The job market for social workers is quite strong—far stronger than for other fields according to predications set by the US Bureau of Labor Statistics (BLS).[2] The BLS expects the job market to increase by 13 percent in the ten-year period between 2019 and 2029. Current estimates show the average annual income for a substance abuse counselor in the United States is $50,470 annually and $24.26 hourly.

There are many ways in which social workers help their communities and many environments in which they work. As a career, the outlook for job opportunities is very good compared with other occupational paths. *Photo_Concepts/iStock/Getty Images.*

Am I Right for a Social Work Career?

So is social work the right career choice for you? This is a tough question to answer because really the answer can only come from you. But don't despair: there are plenty of resources both online and elsewhere that can guide you through the types of questions and considerations that will help you understand the requirements of a particular job and what characteristics and commitments are required to succeed in it. Examples of these are covered in more detail in chapter 2.

there are some generalizations that can be made when it comes to what is most challenging about the job and most gratifying.

Here are some general pros:

- You will have the satisfaction that comes with a job that is challenging, educational, and centered on helping people recover their health and livelihoods free from poverty, health issues, lack of education, domestic abuse, substance abuse problems, or other difficulties.
- The job market is very strong. While it is unfortunate that there is such a need for social workers for various reasons in society, reduced stigma and an increasingly diverse choice of services are helping more people seek the help they need.
- You will have peers and colleagues who share your passion and from whom you can learn.
- There's a vast degree of variety in work environments, from prisons to schools to private practice, to name a few.

And here are some general cons:

- The working hours can be very long and irregular. In some cases, social workers are on call twenty-four hours a day, seven days a week.
- The work is very intensive and can be emotionally and physically draining. You may be confronted with cases that expose you to situations that are violent, high risk, and in some cases disturbing.
- It is a high-pressure field that requires an ability to manage stress as well as to multitask.
- It is a field with a high potential for burnout, and social workers must be on the lookout for signs of a burnout and develop means to keep one at bay.
- Starting your own practice, should you choose that path, can be a difficult and competitive process that will require business skills on top of social work–related education.

> "As an Indigenous social worker, I am trying to indigenize how I practice social work. Anti-Colonial Social Work is my practice. I focus on helping my brothers and sisters learn about our culture and practice healing how it was done before contact. I believe land-based healing and teachings about our traditional medicines can help individuals and communities heal from the years of oppression." —Angela Prince, social worker

FIGHTING FOR WHAT IS RIGHT

Michelle Hominick Anderson.
Courtesy of Michelle Hominick Anderson.

Michelle Hominick Anderson has been a registered social worker since 2008, receiving her BSW in 2009 and MSW in 2015, both from the University of Manitoba. She has worked in a variety of practice settings including a nonprofit NGO focusing on geriatric mental health and addictions, a community hospital emergency department, inpatient and outpatient mental health, an oncology clinic, nursing stations in several First Nations communities under contract with the First Nations and Inuit Health Branch (FNIHB), and private practice, both as an associate and later as a managing partner and therapist. She currently co-owns Floating Bridge Therapy Services, a dialectical behavior therapy (DBT) clinic in Winnipeg, where they specialize in working with people who live with borderline personality disorder (BPD). She is also a field instructor for MSW students and delivers lectures on cognitive behavior therapy (CBT), DBT, BPD, and trauma-informed care.

How did you choose social work as a career?

I remember the day I found social work. I started university believing I was going to be an English teacher. During my first year, I took an Intro to Psychology class, and I was HOOKED! I switched tracks and started taking all the psychology classes I could, focusing mostly on behaviorism and perception. Then, when I was three years into my Honors BA in Psychology, I started feeling that something was missing from all of the courses I was taking. Where was the pursuit of social justice? Where was the heart? I searched on the University of Manitoba website, reviewing the information about a number of faculties, and then I found it—social work had everything that was important to me. I consider it a calling more than a career. If you ask my father, he will tell you I have been fighting for what is right since I could speak. I truly believe I was born to do this work.

Can you describe your educational background and career path to date?

I did my BSW field placement at Jewish Child and Family Services where I learned about CFS policies and procedures, therapy, and community social work. I was the first person to hold the geriatric mental health and addictions role in that agency. I worked there, learning everything I could from the more experienced social workers, for about four years. I applied for a job with Winnipeg Regional Health Authority at Grace Hospital, starting in the Emergency Department. That was the same year I started my MSW, and it took me three years to complete my degree. While I was on maternity leave with my youngest child, I did my MSW practicum at Victoria Hospital on their DBT team and with their inpatient mental health unit, facilitating groups and individual therapy. I think the thing that made me most prepared for the work I do now was finding a way to write every paper and do every assignment on some facet of CBT, wherever possible. The programs didn't provide an opportunity to specialize, so I made my own CBT program.

I worked in various positions at Grace Hospital and got my MSW during my employment there, but when a change in government resulted in what I perceived to be unethical changes in the way the health-care system functioned, particularly the mental health system, I knew it was time to leave. I became a traveling therapist with FNIHB, going up to various FN communities and providing therapy and suicide risk assessments, and I also held an associate contract at a psychology clinic. When COVID hit, the psychology clinic owner chose to shut down, so another associate and I opened our own clinic. I think I always dreamed of opening my own clinic, but I certainly didn't think it would be this soon.

What is a typical day on the job for you?

COVID has resulted in work being anything but "typical." I am incredibly grateful to be in a profession that has been able to continue working virtually through the pandemic. Given it does not appear the COVID workday is going to shift back to pre-COVID anytime soon, I will describe what is typically happening for me now. I live with chronic pain, and it takes me a long time to get moving, so my workday starts at around 10 a.m. I will check e-mails, respond to anything urgent, check for cancellations, and look at who I will see in the day. I pull all the charts I will need and gather any resources that I anticipate using. I typically see five patients a day, all virtually. In between patients, I do the case notes, graze in the kitchen, drink eighty-five cups of coffee, perhaps throw in some laundry, and play with the dogs. My clinic runs two groups per week, and one is in the evening, so that workday is usually ten hours long. We have our DBT team meeting once per week, and I supervise my MSW student(s) once per week. And there is always some kind of paperwork to do with billing and outreach letters or creating forms. When I compare the pace, balance, and satisfaction of my current workday to the type of workday I had while I was working at the hospital, I honestly can't believe I did that for as long as I did. While I will remain forever grateful for everything I learned while I was at the hospital, I know I could never work in an environment like that again. Once we are able to see patients in the clinic, my day will include travel time as I live in the country and probably significantly less laundry and dog petting, though I do crave human interaction and look forward to seeing my coworkers daily.

What's the best or most satisfying part of your job?

The moments when the patient "gets it." When you are working with someone, trying to get them unstuck, over the speed bump they're faced with on their life's journey, and something clicks for them, that feels like magic. Helping people understand how and why they have emotions, and what the heck to do with them when they are there, is incredibly satisfying. It is such an honor to be trusted like this, to receive their stories, to hear about their darkest fears and secrets, and to observe their success as they conquer their goals. We are, each of us, the expert on our own life, and when a patient realizes they are perfectly capable of doing what they need to do in order to help themselves, the shift in their emotional state is palpable. I always tell my patients that my overall goal with them is to ultimately get fired, to which they always laugh, and then I explain that the most satisfying part of my job is working with someone until they no longer need my help and they can achieve their goals and maintain their recovery without me.

What's the most challenging part or stressful part of your job?

All. The. PAPERWORK. Opening up your own clinic means you need to create a document for everything, a policy for everything, learn new things, be very organized, all while trying to do the actual work you want to do, which is to provide therapy to patients. I suppose the good news is that once you create a document, it is done, and you theoretically do not have to redo it for a while. I suppose I just didn't realize the sheer volume of forms and documents that would have to be created, but the good news is that I am in charge of all of this. My managing partner and I are always able to find a synthesis when we have different ideas about what to do, and despite having many responsibilities and commitments, I feel more freedom now than in any other practice setting I have worked in.

What has been the most surprising thing about your job as a social worker?

This is a difficult question to answer. The more patients you work with, the less and less you are surprised by what they say. I would say the times over my career when I have been most surprised are when I witness my fellow social workers not acting in line with our social work values, when I see policy or practice that falls out of line with our code of ethics. I believe and respect our social work values and ethics to the depths of my soul, and I would never feel comfortable doing something or carrying out orders that violated those ethics. Ultimately, as social workers, it is our responsibility to stand up and say something when policy or practice puts our patients at risk, but it is a hard lesson to learn when standing up is ineffective for change or, at worst, gets you into trouble. I think we have to learn to pick our battles, and I think that takes experience over time.

What kinds of qualities and personal attributes do you consider advantageous to doing your job successfully?
I think having a great capacity for empathy is fundamentally important to our profession. Being able to hear what the patient isn't saying and being able to provide critical feedback to them in a way that does not damage your relationship with them is essential. To own a clinic, you must be incredibly dedicated to providing effective treatment, and you have to be able to look at what you are currently doing and identify weak spots for improvement. Operating with an absence of ego, with constant vigilance about how your own vulnerabilities may be impacting on the way you are providing therapy and how your blind spots may be clouding your clinical judgment, is very necessary. As therapists, and as humans, we are fallible and we will make mistakes, and it is crucial to be able to admit these mistakes to your patients and to yourself. I think what I have learned over the years is that I cannot fix anyone, and their recovery is outside the bounds of what I can control—people have to make their own mistakes and help themselves, so letting go of that desire for control is a skill unto itself.

How do you combat burnout?
I think removing myself from a system I no longer believed in was fundamental to addressing my burnout. Nothing burns social workers out more than seeing people in need and feeling totally powerless to help them, whether that powerlessness be due to oppressive policies and procedures of the agency, lack of effective supervision to help you improve your practice, lack of training to provide effective interventions, or anything in between. Goodness of fit between a social worker and the values of the agency in which they work is a good first step to avoiding burnout. Boundaries are essential in this work, and understanding how much of yourself to give to your practice, where your limits are and learning to respect them, is critically important. Personally, I try to be organized so I know what I need to do and when I need to do it, so I don't feel overwhelmed by things piling up. I engage in as much self-care as possible, and when I am tired or in pain, I take a break. I schedule my patients around necessary personal appointments, and I avoid the urge to feel guilty when I simply cannot do everything and see everyone I want to see. While I was at JCFS, I learned a Yiddish expression that roughly translates to: if I am not for myself, who will be for me? It is along the lines of the idea that we cannot pour from an empty cup,

that if we don't take care of ourselves, we cannot effectively help anyone else, and we are the only person who can know when we need self-care. I have carried this idea with me through my whole career to date, and it has yet to fail me.

How do you see your career or the social work field evolving in the future?

As far as the future of my career is concerned, I have many dreams and aspirations for my clinic, and I consider myself very fortunate that my work partner has the same kinds of big ideas. I don't ever see myself moving away from self-employment absolutely, though I have thought of pursuing a PhD in the future should I decide to move out of practice and into teaching at the university. After all, I started university all those years ago hoping to be a teacher, and I very much enjoy the teaching aspects of my work. For now, I am focusing on growing my clinic and trying to provide the most effective service possible.

As far as the future of the social work field is concerned, I have noticed less and less clinical emphasis in the MSW programs I have seen, and this makes me very uneasy. Clinical social work is an important part of the mental health system, and I worry that putting less emphasis on clinical practice in our educational programs will mean insurance companies and agencies will start to become reluctant to cover our services and social workers will be less competitive for fewer clinical jobs. As far as I am concerned, a clinical social worker has the potential to be the most effective mental health clinician available due to our focus on the micro to macro, coupled with our social work ethics, and contributed to by what previously was quite effective clinical training. I am hopeful that educational institutions will offer more clinical training for their MSW students in the future, and I am happy to do what I can to improve this situation by offering clinical MSW placements at my clinic.

Summary

This chapter covered a lot of ground as far as looking more closely at social work as a career and a societal necessity. Social work offers a lot of opportunities for job satisfaction and for having a positive impact. The career outlook for social work is quite strong, with an above average growth prediction that is higher than for many other careers.

Here are some ideas to take away with you as you move on to the next chapter:

- Social work is an exciting and changing field. As societies change and evolve and new challenges and opportunities present themselves, the type of services a social worker can provide will also change and evolve. Societies will always needs social workers to function successfully.
- No two days are alike for a social worker, which makes it an exciting field in which you are continuously challenged and constantly learning.
- As a social worker, you can choose from many different work environments, from schools to prisons to private practices.
- Social workers assist clients from all backgrounds, age groups, socio-economic and geographic circumstances, and career and educational levels. Anyone can require the services of a social worker, from children to veterans, and social workers can serve to resolve individual to community-wide concerns.
- As a profession, social work has a very healthy outlook, with a high percentage of career growth over the next ten years.

Given all you now know about the job and role of a social worker, you may still be questioning whether such a career is right for you. This chapter provided some questions that can help you visualize yourself in real-world situations you can expect to face on the job to help you guide your decision process.

Assuming you are now more enthusiastic than ever about pursuing a career in social work, in the next chapter, we will look more closely at how you can refine your choice to a more specific job. It offers tips and advice on how to find the role and work environment that will be most satisfying to you and what steps you can start taking—immediately!—toward reaching your future career goals.

2

Forming a Career Plan

Choosing a career may seem like one of the most difficult choices you will have to make because it is one of the most important and there are so many options to consider. But it should not feel scary or daunting—it's actually a very exciting thing to think about. Often, it's easy to narrow down what type of careers suit your interests and personality, as we've seen in chapter 1. Other times, you can imagine yourself in many seemingly different careers, which is why it's important to think about what kinds of skills or characteristics or interests are at the root of your career ambitions.

There are simply so many types of careers out there, and it is easy to feel overwhelmed. Particularly if you have many passions and interests, it can be hard to narrow your options down. If "helping people and making a difference" rank high on your list of qualities of a job that appeals to you, then social work is definitely worth looking into, and that you are reading this book means you have decided to investigate a career in the field more closely.

You have hopefully already discovered a passion for promoting change for good, working to resolve societal issues, encouraging health and well-being, effective communication, and continuous learning, and social work checks these boxes. But even within the social work field, there are many types of jobs to choose from. Considerations include what role you want to pursue, in what environment you desire to work, and what type of work schedule best fits your lifestyle.

It's a lot to think about, but fortunately it's also very exciting to consider your options, particularly as it's a decision that is primarily based on aspects of you (your interests, natural gifts, curiosities) that you know more about than anyone else.

A career in social work is in some ways a very specific choice of career, but it also offers a lot of choice and variety as far as who your clients are, what issues you want to help address, in what environment you will work, and how you

> **Tip:** This may all sound very overwhelming. Keep in mind as you consider your career options that it is common to change your mind or shift gears at any stage in your career. Be thoughtful about your decisions, but don't put too much pressure on yourself. It's not a case of only getting one chance to decide.

can contribute to the field through research or working directly with clients and their families and the communities in which they live.

Before you can plan the path to a successful career in the social work field—such as by committing to a college program—it's helpful to develop an understanding of what role you want to have and in what environment you wish to work. Do you want to work in an established organization, or do you prefer the more entrepreneurial feel of a private practice? Do you want to work specifically with young people? Or maybe you want to focus on researching new approaches to combating education or financial inequalities. Are you willing to relocate for your job or work long hours and weekends? These are all things to consider.

Also important to think about: how much education would you like to pursue? Depending on your ultimate career goal, the steps to getting there differ. Jobs in social work will typically require a bachelor's degree or higher, and specific certifications may be required before you can practice. You can choose to study anything that relates to social work, such as behavioral science, psychology, sociology, law, education, medicine, or a program in social work. The choices are many, and we will look at them a bit in this chapter, as well as discuss particular schools that offer programs of interest.

Deciding on a career means asking yourself big questions, but there are several tools and assessment tests that can help you determine what your personal strengths and aptitudes are and with which career fields and environments they

> **Note:** Clinical social work, which is the type of job many people think about when they hear the term "social work," is centered on individual and group or family therapy and focused on assessing, diagnosing, and treating mental illness or emotional and behavioral problems. If you want to pursue this career path in social work, you will be required to earn a master's degree in the majority of cases.

> **YOUR PASSIONS, ABILITIES, AND INTERESTS: IN JOB FORM!**
>
> Think about how you've done at school and how things have worked out at any temporary or part-time jobs you've had so far. What are you really good at, in your opinion? And what have other people told you you're good at? What are you not very good at right now but you would like to become better at? What are you not very good at and you're okay with not getting better at?
>
> Now forget about work for a minute. In fact, forget about needing to ever have a job again. You won the lottery—congratulations. Now answer these questions: What are your favorite three ways of spending your time? For each one of those things, can you describe why you think you in particular are attracted to it? If you could get up tomorrow and do anything you wanted all day long, what would it be? These questions can be fun but can also lead you to your true passions. The next step is to find the job that sparks your passions.

best align. These tools guide you to think about important factors in choosing a career path, such as how you respond to pressure and how effectively—and how much you enjoy—working and communicating with people. These will be discussed in this chapter as well.

This chapter explores the educational requirements for various careers within the social work field, as well as options for where to go for help when planning your path to the career you want. It offers advice on how to begin preparing for your career path at any age or stage in your education, including in high school.

Planning the Plan

So where to begin? Before taking the leap and applying to or committing in your mind to a particular college or program, there are other considerations and steps you can take to map out your plan for pursing your career. Preparing your career plan begins with developing a clear understanding of what your actual career goal is.

Planning your career path means asking yourself questions that will help shape a clearer picture of what your long-term career goals are and what steps to take in order to achieve them. When considering these questions, it's important to prioritize your answers—when listing your skills, for example, put them in order of strongest to weakest. When considering questions relating to how you want to balance your career with the rest of your nonwork life, such as family and hobbies, really think about what your top priorities are and in what order.

The following are questions that are helpful to think about deeply when planning your career path.

- Think about your interests outside of the work context. How do you like to spend your free time? What inspires you? What kind of people do you like to surround yourself with, and how do you best learn? What do you really love doing? (Hint: If you find you are impatient when others discuss their personal problems or if you are not interested in keeping up with societal issues and the people they affect, social work may not be for you!)
- Brainstorm a list of the various career choices within the social work/helping others/community service arena that you are interested in pursuing (think about whether you are interested in protecting vulnerable people; in politics, education, health, or economics; and in tackling societal issues). Organize the list in order of which careers you find most appealing, and then list what it is about each that attracts you. This can be anything from work environment to geographical location to the degree to which you would work with other people in a particular role.
- Research information on each job on your career choices list. You can find job descriptions, salary indications, career outlook, and educational requirements information online, for example. Some of this information was provided in chapter 1 of this book.
- Consider your personality traits. This is very important to finding which jobs "fit" you and which almost certainly do not. How do you respond to stress and pressure? Do you consider yourself a strong communicator? Do you work well in teams or prefer to work independently? Do you consider yourself a creative thinker? How do you respond to criticism? Are you curious and thorough? All of these are important to keep in mind to ensure you choose a career path that makes you happy and in which you can thrive.
- Although a career choice is obviously a huge factor in your future, it's important to consider what other factors feature in your vision of your

ideal life. Think about how your career will fit in with the rest of your life, including whether you want to live in a big city or small town, how much flexibility you want in your schedule, how much autonomy you want in your work, and what your ultimate career goal is.
- The job of social work is a sensitive one that carries some high stakes: helping a person modify their behaviors that are sabotaging their health, well-being, and relationships; working to combat the negative influences of people or institutions in position of power; alleviating the struggles of individuals who are vulnerable. Wherever you work and whomever you advocate for, your role will be to guide a client through their problem-solving and often recovery journey, which will likely entail crises and struggles along the way.
- Some of the most fulfilling and meaningful work can also be the most taxing emotionally and physically, demanding long and irregular hours. Because succeeding in the social work field requires so much commitment, it's important to think about how willing you are to put in long hours and perform what can be very demanding work—without burning out.

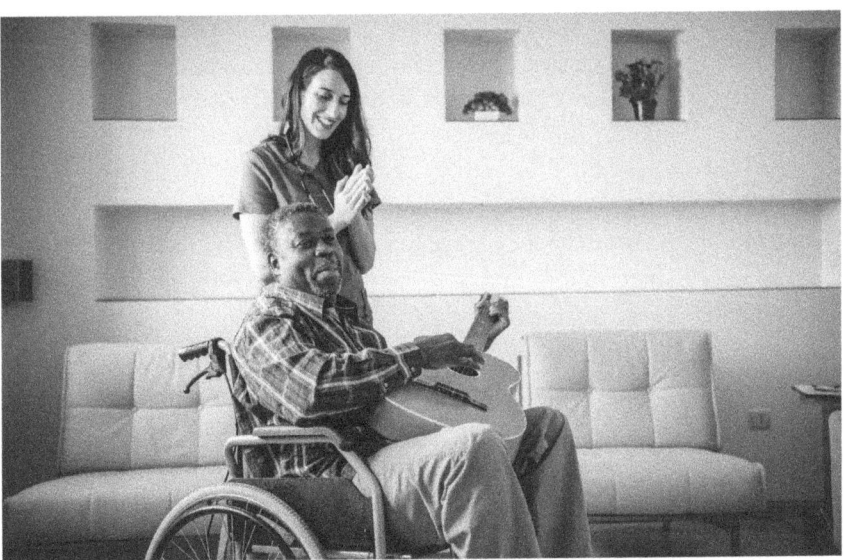

Although the job of a social worker can often be stressful and emotionally tiring if not difficult, it also brings with it the opportunity to connect deeply with other people and the satisfaction of engaging with others and helping improve their circumstances, whatever they are. *RealPeopleGroup/E+/Getty Images.*

- Many job opportunities that offer experience to newcomers and recent graduates can come with relatively low salaries. What are your pay expectations, now and in the future?

Posing these questions to yourself and thinking about them deeply and answering them honestly will help make your career goals clearer and guide you in knowing which steps you will need to take to get there.

Where to Go for Help

Again, the process of deciding on and planning a career path can be a little bit daunting. In many ways, the range of choices of careers available today is a wonderful thing. It allows us to refine our career goals and customize them to our own lives and personalities. In other ways, though, too much choice can be extremely confusing and require a lot of soul searching to navigate clearly.

> **Note:** Depending on your age and educational level, you might also be thinking you have time to consider these points more carefully. But the sooner you start thinking in terms of a particular career path, the better prepared you will be to spot opportunities that present themselves in your schooling or your life to advance your relative skill sets.

Answering questions about your habits, preferences, interests, and personality can be very hard to do—and to do honestly. Identifying and prioritizing all of your ambitions, interests, and passions is tough. It's not always easy to see ourselves objectively or see a way to achieve what matters most to us. But there are several resources and approaches to help guide you in drawing conclusions about these important questions.

- Take a career assessment test to help you answer questions about what career best suits you. There are several available online, which you can find via your search engine.
- Consult with a career or personal coach to help you refine your understanding of your goals and how to pursue them.

WHAT IS THE DIFFERENCE BETWEEN A COUNSELOR AND A SOCIAL WORKER?

The same reasons and interests that draw a person to social work as a career may well make a future in counseling appealing. This can mean individual therapy (or group or family) for a variety of issues, including addiction and mental health struggles. As both careers involve helping people by diagnosing, treating, and managing an issue they are confronting, it might be difficult to decide which path is for you or to understand how they are different.

The requirements for both careers are similar: both require degrees and programs and both involve mandatory field work (working directly with actual clients). Both demand similar skills, such as problem-solving and communication skills. The main difference is in scope. Generally speaking, the role of a counselor tends to have a more narrow focus, working with individuals and family members on behavioral, emotional, and mental health, while social workers aid clients in navigating the often complicated world of social services, which support those in need with access to such necessities as education or health care.

As far as educational paths go, if you are deciding between a degree in social work and a degree in counseling, the main difference will be that the social work degree will prepare candidates for working within broad societal contexts while the emphasis in a counseling program will be more on understanding human behavior and development.

So while there is a lot of overlap in the functions of a counselor and a social worker, the two occupations and the educational and job-preparation pathways to becoming one or the other differ in key ways.

- Talk with professionals working in the job you are considering and ask them what they enjoy about their work, what they find the most challenging, and what path they followed to get there.
- Educate yourself as much as possible about the field. What are the latest research breakthroughs or trends in social work or in the particular "problem areas" on which you are interested in focusing? What are the latest statistics about substance abuse problems or poor housing or other issues being faced by people in the United States and beyond? Stay current as much as possible with topics relating to the career you wish to pursue.

- Although for privacy reasons it may not be possible to "job shadow" a social worker—accompany someone during their workday to witness firsthand what a typical day on the job is like—you can likely arrange to visit a treatment center or hospital to get a sense of the environment.

ONLINE RESOURCES TO HELP YOU PLAN YOUR PATH

The Internet is an excellent source of advice and assessment tools that can help you find and figure out how to pursue your career path. Some of these tools focus on an individual's personality and aptitude; others can help you identify and improve your skills to prepare for your career.

In addition to these sites below, you can use the Internet to find a career or life coach near you—many offer their services online as well. Job sites such as LinkedIn are a good place to search for people working in a profession you'd like to learn more about or to explore the types of jobs available in social work.

- At educations.com, you will find a career test designed to help you find the job of your dreams. Visit https://www.educations.com/career-test to take the test.
- The Princeton Review has created a career quiz that focuses on personal interests: https://www.princetonreview.com/quiz/career-quiz.
- To specifically discover whether you should become a social worker, check out Grizly.com, which offers a one-minute online quiz: https://grizly.com/quizzes/social-worker-quiz/.
- Find out what kind of social worker you should be with the help of this quiz from the National Association of Social Workers: https://www.socialworkers.org/Careers/NASW-Career-Center/Explore-Social-Work/What-Type-of-Social-Worker-Will-You-Be.
- The US Bureau of Labor Statistics provides information, including quizzes and videos, to help students up to grade twelve explore various career paths. The site also provides general information on career prospects and salaries. Visit BLS.gov to find these resources.

FORMING A CAREER PLAN

Note: Young adults with disabilities can face additional challenges when planning a career path. DO-IT (Disabilities, Opportunities, Internetworking, and Technology) is an organization dedicated to promoting career and education inclusion for everyone. Its website contains a wealth of information and tools to help all young people plan a career path, including self-assessment tests and career exploration questionnaires: https://www.washington.edu/doit/preparing-career-online-tutorial.

Making High School Count

Once you have narrowed down your interests and have a fairly solid idea what type of career you want to pursue, you naturally want to start putting your career path plan into motion as quickly as you can. If you are a high school student, you may feel there isn't much you can do toward achieving your career goals—other than, of course, earning good grades and graduating.

Even while still in high school, there are many ways you can begin working toward your career goal. Classes in another language, in writing, in interpersonal communication, and in health can all help you prepare for a career as a social worker. *skynesher/E+/Getty Images.*

But there are actually many ways you can make your high school years count toward your career in social work before you have earned your high school diploma. This section will cover how you can use this period of your education and life to better prepare you for your career goal and to ensure you keep your passion alive while improving your skill set.

COURSES TO TAKE IN HIGH SCHOOL

Depending on your high school and what courses are offered and that you have access to, there are many subjects that will help you prepare for a career in social work. Beyond doing your own research into different areas of social work and different work environments and the types of clients you may serve in the future, you can take advantage of any college prep courses your school offers, particularly in areas relating to psychology or sociology but also in subjects such as public speaking or literature to help you strengthen your communication skills.

> **Tip:** Everybody harbors biases in the way they think about sensitive issues such as race and sexual identity. To find out whether you have biases of which you may be unaware, check out this text online, which was developed at Harvard University: https://implicit.harvard.edu/implicit/takeatest.html.

Here are some courses that you should pursue while in high school. Some of them may seem unrelated initially, but they will all help you prepare yourself and develop key skills.

- **Math:** Research requires an understanding of math, including how to interpret statistics and percentages—and to put them into terms you, your colleagues, a client, and a client's family will understand.
- **Interpersonal communication/public speaking:** These courses will be an asset in any profession but especially in social work. You will be communicating with many other people when working with clients; doing so effectively will be a major factor in your success.
- **A second language:** To expand your clientele and be able to reach more people in need of a social worker, learning a second language will be a great asset.

SOCIAL WORK EDUCATION WITH AN EMPHASIS ON RACIAL JUSTICE

The goal of all social work practice should be to ensure individuals everywhere from all backgrounds and stages in life are able to live safely and with access to basics such as food, water, shelter, and education. Social work is in a very real sense about human rights, which means protecting key principles: human dignity, nondiscrimination, participation, transparency, and accountability.

It is important to ensure that, at an educational level, these principles are engrained in all people entering the social work field by those in the position of teaching them. The following tips on how to ensure antiracist practices in social work college-level teaching were shared in a blog post by Dr. Laurel Hitchcock, a professor and licensed social worker (these have been paraphrased):[1]

- Learn about the history of social work and teach more history in the classroom. Historically, many social work programs were designed to "aid" Black, Indigenous, and other people of color (BIPOC) assimilate to a "whiter" society. Teaching this history is important because social workers need to be able to respect and understand the communities they are trying to support.
- In social work, as in any profession, it is important to be aware of the existence and impact of systemic racism—racist thinking that is embedded in regulations or laws. Be alert to any approaches to social work that can lead to discrimination.
- As always, be aware of your own biases that you may have and not even fully realize when it comes to thinking about people of races, religions, cultural backgrounds, economic backgrounds, or sexual orientations other than your own.
- Be inclusive in the people you work for and with and in those you learn from either through research or life experience.
- Always work to provide a safe environment for everyone. This sounds obvious perhaps, but it requires being aware that certain experiences of trauma—abuse, neglect, violence—can sustain and affect individuals and communities, and you should avoid triggering these negative feelings however possible in your work.

> **Tip:** Taking advanced placement (AP) courses while in high school (assuming you pass the AP exam at the end of the course) may enable you to earn college credit early and skip taking an elementary or introductory course in the subject (for example, psychology) when you get to college.

- **Business and economics:** If you imagine yourself running a private practice, you will need to have business and accounting skills as well as those required to be a qualified social worker.

GAINING WORK EXPERIENCE

The best way to learn anything is to do it. When it comes to preparing for a career in social work or any type of community service or advocacy, you can consider volunteering in your community, school, or church.

Volunteering in this way will provide you valuable training in areas such as recognizing problems and ways in which people can make the world a better place in large and small ways for others. It will also help you improve the qualities of an effective social worker, such as patience, compassion, and good listening and communication skills.

Find out if your school offers any opportunities for volunteering, such as a peer counseling group or community service opportunities. You can also contact local health clinics, libraries, community centers, and other organizations to seek out volunteer opportunities there. There are so many ways volunteers help individuals and communities—food drives, cleaning up parks, tutoring children, doing errands for older people—and all of these initiatives will help prepare you for a career in social work.

Educational Requirements

You will have to pursue post-high-school education in order to become a social worker. The level of post-high-school degree you pursue is up to you—but keep in mind the higher a degree you earn, the better your chances are at securing employment and earning a higher salary.

HOW SOCIAL WORKERS PRACTICE "SELF-CARE"

This book has already touched on the fact that despite social work being a job that carries with it an undeniable "feel-good" factor, meaning it brings feelings of positivity and satisfaction, it also can be physically and emotionally draining. "Self-care" refers to the various ways people can ensure that they are looking after their own needs, eating and sleeping well, for example, or taking exercise to release energy and process thoughts in a healthy, beneficial way. Doing so can help anyone, but especially social workers and others in similar professions, maintain their own sense of well-being so they are better prepared and able to help others and avoid burnout.

The following tips for social workers on how to practice self-care are provided by licensed social worker Jane E. Shersher:[2]

1. Focus on your breathing. Take long, slow, deep breaths as a way of maintaining your calm and relaxing your mind. Consider setting a timer to remind yourself to breathe in this way a few times a day for a minute or two at a time. It may sound a little strange to remind yourself to breathe, but doing so in this manner can lead to noticeable results.
2. Do a body scan. This might also sound a bit odd, but you can help your body and mind relax by paying attention to each body part one at a time from head to toe, concentrating on it and checking for points of tension to release.
3. Use guided imagery. Visualize yourself in a place or an environment that helps to calm you down, inspire you, or aid you in focusing for stretches of time (a few minutes, for example). There are apps you can use to help you feel calm, such as apps that you can use to listen to soothing sounds, such as nature sounds.
4. Practice mindfulness. Mindfulness has certainly gained in popularity over the past several years. It is the practice of focusing your awareness on the present moment, while noticing and accepting feelings, thoughts, and bodily sensations. There are several apps that offer guided mindfulness meditations that you can try.
5. Practice yoga, tai chi, or qigong. These are physical exercises for the body and mind that help with mental focus, flexibility, and balance and can reduce anxiety. You can incorporate these several times a day.
6. Get enough sleep. Sleep is so important; it cannot be stressed enough. Your body should be getting, on average, seven to eight hours of sleep. Try to build a routine that helps you be able to fall into a sleepy state so you can have a restful night. Exercise, diet, and winding-down routines (like taking a bath, reading a book) can help.

Whatever type of job you want to pursue in social work, you should expect to have to earn at minimum a two-year associate's degree to introduce you to the career and help you decide if you want to go further and earn a four-year bachelor's degree, which is recommended for social work careers. In other cases, a master's or even a PhD is recommended. In addition, there are certificates you can earn at your community college or online to continue or broaden your education throughout your career.

> **Note:** Realistically speaking, in order to achieve the highest level of success, be competitive for the best opportunities, and make the strongest impact with a social work career, you should consider completing a master's degree. But keep in mind, many people earn a master's degree after spending some time working full-time in their chosen field. It's very common for professionals to earn degrees while working full- or part-time, and in some cases employers offer financial assistance or work-hour flexibility in order to help valuable staff pursue advanced education.

HOW TO PREPARE FOR RUNNING A PRIVATE SOCIAL WORK PRACTICE

Although this chapter has already provided advice on the types of courses you should consider taking in high school or higher education to help prepare you for success as a social worker, if you have the ambition to run your own private practice, you will gain from taking even more business-related courses.

Running a business is its own challenge, on top of that of becoming a qualified social worker. Mastering certain business skills is absolutely crucial to succeeding in running your own practice, from doing your own accounting to getting the word out to attract clients. Here are some general tips for preparing to launch your own practice as a social worker:

1. **Accounting:** Take a lower-division accounting course. You will be responsible for managing the money for your business, and therefore, you will need to understand basic accounting concepts.
2. **Advertising:** Seek out courses that deal with the topic of advertising and promotion. If your campus does not offer any, look into online classes that

would be convenient and time-efficient. Consider it a hobby instead of another class. Topics that will be helpful are ones that deal with promotional design, cost-effective advertising techniques, and anything else that will help your business become prominent in the public eye.

3. **Social media marketing:** Today's professional doesn't just rely on word of mouth, business cards, and a nicely painted sign to increase the traffic flow of their business. Savvy social workers have mastered the world of Twitter, LinkedIn, Google+, Facebook, and other social media. You may already have these skills under your belt, so begin to think in terms of how to effectively integrate them into the realm of a private social work practice. Begin to look at other social workers who are involved in marketing themselves through social media channels, and notice what you like and what changes you would make. Have fun with this—your imagination is your friend.

4. **Business plan:** Anyone planning on success has some concept of what it means to devise a business plan. Basically this is a well-researched, well-thought-out document that analyzes costs and projected income. You will need a business plan if you intend to seek out a loan from a bank and/or investor. If your college has a business major, go to the department offices and inquire as to the classes that might be appropriate for your endeavors. If this is not available or practical, begin to read online about what a business plan is and how to come up with one. Even if you do not plan on securing financial backing, a wise business owner always has a plan.

5. **Minor in business:** If you are convinced you will want to go into private practice, you might consider choosing business as your minor. It may sound like something you really do not want to do. However, if you go into private practice, it will be a fact that you will be doing business on a daily basis.

6. **Seminars on small business:** During your quarter or semester breaks, consider attending a small-business seminar. It will be a fast and easy way to get some basics under your belt; it will also give you a heads-up on what might lie ahead.

7. **Web design course:** Depending on finances, you may end up having to design a simple website for your practice. But even if you plan on hiring someone else to do it, knowing what you're paying for is always smart business. Find out what attracts the eye and what doesn't. Discover what appeals to different age groups and target your clientele.

> "[I love the] moments when the patient 'gets it.' When you are working with someone, trying to get them unstuck, over the speed bump they're faced with on their life's journey, and something clicks for them, that feels like magic. Helping people understand how and why they have emotions, and what the heck to do with them when they are there, is incredibly satisfying. It is such an honor to be trusted like this, to receive their stories, to hear about their darkest fears and secrets, and to observe their success as they conquer their goals." —Michelle Hominick Anderson, registered social worker and addiction counselor

WHY CHOOSE AN ASSOCIATE'S DEGREE?

You may be tempted to pursue an associate's degree after earning your high school diploma. This degree takes comparably shorter time and course work to complete, as related to other advanced degrees you might consider, and if you are living near a community college, that adds a layer of convenience.

A two-year degree—called an associate's degree—is sufficient to give you a knowledge base to begin your career and can form as a basis should you decide to pursue a four-year degree later. Do keep in mind, though, that jobs in social work are quite competitive. If you are prepared to put in the financial and time commitment to earn an associate's degree and are sure of the career goal you have set for yourself, consider earning a bachelor's instead. With so much competition out there, the more of an edge you can give yourself, the better your chances will be.

WHY CHOOSE A BACHELOR'S DEGREE?

A bachelor's degree—which usually takes four years to acquire—is a requirement in most cases for a career in social work. And in general, the higher the education you pursue, the better your odds are to advance in your career, which means more opportunity and often more compensation.

The difference between an associate's and a bachelor's degree is of course the amount of time each takes to complete. To earn a bachelor's degree, a candidate must complete forty college credits, compared with twenty for an associate's. This translates to more courses completed and a deeper exploration of degree content, even though similar content is covered in both.

FORMING A CAREER PLAN

> **Note:** Even when not required, continuing your education as far as possible can help advance your career, give you an edge over the competition in the field, and give you more specific knowledge relating to your work in social work.

WHY CHOOSE A MASTER'S DEGREE?

A master's degree is an advanced degree that usually takes two years to complete. A master's will offer you a chance to become more specialized and to build on the education and knowledge you gained while earning your bachelor's. A master's can be done directly after your bachelor's, although many people choose to work for a while in between in order to discover what type of master's degree is most relevant to their careers and interests. Many people also earn their master's degree while working full- or part-time.

> **Note:** In some instances, a PhD will be required, depending on your career goals. If you have the desire to teach or perform research at the university level, you will be required to hold a PhD in a relevant subject.

"SOCIAL WORK CHOSE ME"

Angela Prince. *Courtesy of Angela Prince.*

Angela Prince is a bachelor of social work grad from the University of Manitoba. She is currently working on her grad studies through the University of Manitoba to earn a master's of social work with an emphasis on Indigenous knowledge. Angela grew up in a small town in southern Manitoba, separated from her father; Angela decided to move to Winnipeg, where she later married and raised a family. Through years of unrecognized systematic oppression, Angela decided to uncover the truth of her Indigenous ancestors. She made the career choice to become a social worker to give back and be of assistance to those suffering and needing to navigate the area of systemic oppression.

How did you choose social work as a career?

Social work chose me. During my middle school and high school years, I was a peer mentor. I helped listen to my friends and provide support when they were dealing with personal and individual difficulties. At an early age, I understood that I would be in the helping profession and eventually starting my own business and making a career out of it. I married at a young age and had children in my twenties while attending school part-time to achieve my bachelor's degree. During my studies, I remained employed as a support worker for Indigenous children in the Child Welfare System's custody.

Can you describe your educational background and career path to date?

By the time I was thirty, I had achieved a bachelor's degree in social work. I was employed in Child and Family Services for twelve years. I worked as a direct services worker, foster care resource worker, and child abuse investigator. By age forty-two, I resigned from Child and Family Services. I began providing counseling for Indigenous Services Canada as a contract mental health therapist. During this past year of surviving a global pandemic, I enrolled in the Master's of Social Work Program—Indigenous Knowledge through the University of Manitoba. I continue to practice social work part-time and on the weekends.

What is a typical day on the job for you?

As a mental health therapist, I travel to remote communities in northern Manitoba over the weekends to help with service delivery. I schedule clients to come in and talk with me and discuss whatever issues are troubling them. A typical workday would typically be from 9 a.m. to 5 p.m.; however, you have to be flexible and provide support when needed.

What's the best or most satisfying part of your job?

The best part of my job is building relationships with community members. The most satisfying part of my job is witnessing people make a change and live a healthy and purposeful life.

What's the most challenging part or stressful part of your job?

The most challenging part of my job is the unseen, unrecognizable colonial oppression Indigenous people face. This systematic oppression can result in a life of addictions and trauma. Challenges arise when people do not recognize that addiction and trauma affect the entire community. Working through years of colonial trauma is a process, and habits have been pathologized to make individuals think that they have to deal with their addictions alone. Community programming and support are essential.

What has been the most surprising thing about your job as a social worker?

Nothing surprises me. I grew up as an Indigenous child in a predominantly non-Indigenous community due to my father being a product of the sixties scoop. My grandmother was a residential school survivor. The trauma was already there through the years and affected our family. Working in the social work field, I understood the impacts. I just did not understand the cause.

What kinds of qualities and personal attributes do you consider advantageous to doing your job successfully?

Social work is not for those that want to hold power over anyone. Individual strength and growth are what make a great social worker. Years of practice and knowledge do not create a good social worker if you do not have empathy and a will to help others.

How do you combat burnout?

Self-care is critical. As a social worker, you will burn out. It is inevitable, but all social workers understand the impact that helping others can have on themselves. Being able to release and let go of the vicarious trauma that social workers carry is important. Healthy outlets for release are necessary. Connecting with the traditional and cultural ceremony is also a healthy outlet for individual self-care, including meditation and prayer. As an Indigenous social worker, I am trying to indigenize how I practice social work. Anti-colonial social work is my practice. I focus on helping my brothers and sisters learn about our culture and practice healing how it was done before contact. I believe land-based healing and teachings about our traditional medicines can help individuals and communities heal from the years of oppression.

Summary

This chapter covered a lot of ground in terms of how to break down the challenge of not only discovering whether a career as a social worker is right for you and in what environment, capacity, and work culture you want to work, but also how best to prepare yourself for achieving your career goal.

In this chapter, you learned about some of the specific training and educational options and requirements and expectations that will put you, no matter what your current education level or age, at a strong advantage in a competitive field.

Use this chapter as a guideline for how to best discover what type of career will be the right fit for you and consider what steps you can already be taking to get there. Some tips to leave you with:

- Take time to carefully consider what kind of work environment you see yourself working in and what kind of schedule, interaction with colleagues, work culture, and responsibilities you want to have.
- Pay attention to current research and issues relating to social problems to stay abreast of trends and important statistics in the field of social work.
- Talk with a professional to get a feeling for what hours they keep, what challenges they face, and what the overall job entails. Find out what education or training they completed before launching their career.
- Investigate various colleges and certification options so you can better prepare yourself for the next step in your career path (more on this in chapter 3).
- Don't feel you have to wait until you graduate from high school to begin taking steps to accomplish your career goals.
- Keep work/life balance in mind. The career you choose will be one of many adult decisions you make, and ensuring that you keep all of your priorities—family, location, work schedule—in mind will help you choose the right career for you, which will make you a happier person.

In chapter 3, we go into detail about the next steps—writing a résumé and cover letter, interviewing well, follow-up communications, and more. This is information you can use to secure internships, volunteer positions, summer jobs, and so on. It's not just for college grads. In fact, the sooner you can hone these skills, the better off you'll be in the professional world.

3

Pursuing the Education Path

Making decisions about your educational path can be just as complex a process as choosing a career in the first place. It is a decision that not only demands understanding what kind of education or training is required for the career you want but also what kind of school or college you want to attend and, of course, how you are going to pay for it. Everyone has different circumstances that need to be taken into consideration, be they geographical or economical. There is a lot to consider no matter what area of study you want to pursue and what type of job you want to have within the field of social work.

Now that you've gotten an overview of the different degree options that can prepare you for your future career as a social worker, this chapter will dig more deeply into how to best choose the right type of study plan for you. Even if you are years away from earning your high school diploma or equivalent, it's never too soon to start weighing your options, thinking about the application process, and of course taking time to really consider what kind of educational track and environment will suit you best.

Not everyone wants to take time to go to college or pursue additional academic-based training, and for many careers, it is not required, even if recommended. However, a career in social work will require some level of higher education after you earn your high school degree or equivalent. It is not a field you can enter without earning certain qualifications.

So if you are interested in and prepared to follow the post-high-school (or advanced) educational path, this chapter will help you navigate the process of deciding on the type of institution you would most thrive in, determining what type of degree you want to earn, and looking into costs and how to find help in meeting them.

The chapter will also give you advice on the application process, how to prepare for any entrance exams such as the SAT or ACT that you may need to take, and how to communicate your passion, ambition, and personal

> **Note:** At the time of writing, the United States and beyond are coming out of a pandemic that has caused some of the traditional approaches to teaching and learning to change—hopefully just temporarily. This chapter is offering advice that assumes you will be applying to and attending educational institutions in person, which will hopefully be the case. Even if the way you engage with institutions, faculty members, or other students is a bit unorthodox, the advice offered here is still relevant.

experience in a personal statement. When you've completed this chapter, you should have a good sense of what kind of post-high-school education is right for you and how to ensure you have the best chance of being accepted at the institution of your choice.

Finding a Program or School That Fits Your Personality

Before we get into the details of good schools that offer degrees in subjects related to social work, it's a good idea for you to take some time to consider what "type" of school will be best for you. Just as with your future work environment, understanding how you best learn, what type of atmosphere best fits your personality, and how and where you are most likely to succeed will play a major part in how happy you will be with your choice. This section will provide some thinking points to help you refine what kind of school or program is the best fit for you.

If nothing else, answering questions like the following ones can help you narrow your search and focus on a smaller sampling of choices. Write your answers to these questions down somewhere where you can refer to them often, such as in the notes app on your phone:

- **Size:** Does the size of the school matter to you? Colleges and universities range from sizes of five hundred or fewer students to twenty-five thousand students. If you are considering college or university, think about what size of class you would like and what the right instructor-to-student ratio is for you.

CONSIDERING A GAP YEAR

Taking a year off between high school and college, often called a gap year, is normal, perfectly acceptable, and even increasingly seen as a strong enhancement to a college application. Particularly if you want to pursue a career as a social worker, having exposure to the world outside of the classroom will help you gain perspective and experience that you can immediately apply to your future work. It can help you become more empathic, less judgmental, and a more open thinker. Because the cost of college has gone up dramatically, it literally pays for you to know going in what you want to study, and a gap year—well spent—can do lots to help you answer that question. It can also give you an opportunity to explore different places and people to help you find a deeper sense of what you'd like to study when your gap year has ended.

Some great ways to spend your gap year include joining the Peace Corps or other organizations that offer opportunities for work experience. A gap year can help you see things from a new perspective. Consider enrolling in a mountaineering program or other gap-year-styled program, backpacking across Europe or other countries on the cheap (be safe and bring a friend), finding a volunteer organization that furthers a cause you believe in or that complements your career aspirations, joining a Road Scholar program (see www.roadscholar.org), or teaching English in another country (see https://www.gooverseas.com/blog/best-countries-for-seniors-to-teach-english-abroad for more information), or work and earn money for college!

Many students will find that they get much more out of college when they have a year to mature and to experience the real world. The American Gap Year Association reports from their alumni surveys that students who take gap years show improved civic engagement, improved college graduation rates, and improved GPAs in college.

See their website at https://gapyearassociation.org/ for lots of advice and resources if you're considering a potentially life-altering experience.

- **Community location:** Would you prefer to be in a rural area, a small town, a suburban area, or a large city? How important is the location of the school in the larger world to you? Is the flexibility of an online degree or certification program attractive to you, or do you prefer more on-site, hands-on instruction?
- **Length of study:** How many months or years do you want to put into your education before you start working professionally?

- **Housing options:** If applicable, what kind of housing would you prefer? Dorms, off-campus apartments, and private homes are all common options.
- **Student body:** How would you like the student body to "look"? Think about coed versus all-male and all-female settings, as well as the makeup of minorities, how many students are part-time versus full-time, and the percentage of commuter students.
- **Academic environment:** Consider which majors are offered and at which levels of degree. Research the student-faculty ratio. Are the classes taught often by actual professors or more often by the teaching assistants? Find out how many internships the school typically provides to students. Are independent study or study abroad programs available in your area of interest?
- **Financial aid availability/cost:** Does the school provide ample opportunities for scholarships, grants, work-study programs, and the like? Does cost play a role in your options? (For most people, it does.)
- **Support services:** Investigate the strength of the academic and career placement counseling services of the school.
- **Social activities and athletics:** Does the school offer clubs that you are interested in? Which sports are offered? Are scholarships available?
- **Specialized programs:** Does the school offer honors programs or programs for veterans or students with disabilities or special needs?

> **Note:** Not all of these questions are going to be important to you and that's fine. Be sure to make note of aspects that don't matter so much to you too, such as size or location. You might change your mind as you go to visit colleges, but it's important to make note of where you are to begin with.

U.S. News & World Report puts it best when they say the college that fits you best is one that will do all these things:[1]

- offer a degree that matches your interests and needs,
- provide a style of instruction that matches the way you like to learn,
- provide a level of academic rigor to match your aptitude and preparation,
- offer a community that feels like home to you, and
- value you for what you do well.

MAKE THE MOST OF CAMPUS VISITS

If it's at all practical and feasible, you should visit the campuses of all the schools you're considering. To get a real feel for any college or university, you need to walk around the campus, spend some time in the common areas where students hang out, and sit in on a few classes. You can also sign up for campus tours, which are typically given by current students. This is another good way to see the campus and ask questions of someone who knows. Be sure to visit the specific school/building that covers your possible major as well. The website and brochures won't be able to convey that tangible feeling you'll get from a visit.

In addition to the questions listed previously, consider these questions as well. Make a list of questions that are important to you before you visit.

- What is the makeup of the current freshman class? Is the campus diverse?
- What is the meal plan like? What are the food options?
- Where do most of the students hang out between classes? (Be sure to visit this area.)
- How long does it take to walk from one end of the campus to the other?
- What types of transportation are available for students? Does campus security provide escorts to cars, dorms, and so forth at night?

In order to be ready for your visit and make the most of it, consider these tips and words of advice:

- Be sure to do some research. At the least, spend some time on the college website. Make sure your questions aren't addressed adequately there first.
- Make a list of questions.
- Arrange to meet with a professor in your area of interest or to visit the specific school.
- Be prepared to answer questions about yourself and why you are interested in this school.
- Dress in neat, clean, and casual clothes. Avoid overly wrinkled clothing or anything with stains.
- Listen and take notes.
- Don't interrupt.
- Be positive and energetic.
- Make eye contact when someone speaks directly to you.
- Ask questions.
- Thank people for their time.
- Send thank-you notes or e-mails after the visit is over. Remind the recipient when you visited the campus and thank them for their time.

> **Note:** As mentioned earlier, given the current coronavirus pandemic, it is possible you will attend many of your courses online. However, many of the points will still apply, such as the student-to-professor ratio and the diversity of the student body.

The aim of this section has been to impress upon you the importance of finding the right fit for your chosen learning institution. Take some time to paint a mental picture about the kind of university or school setting that will best complement your needs. Then read on for specifics about each degree.

> **Note:** In the academic world, accreditation matters and is something you should consider when choosing a school. Accreditation is basically a seal of approval that schools promote to let prospective students feel sure the institution will provide a quality education that is worth the investment and will help graduates reach their career goals. Future employers will want to see that the program you completed has such a seal of quality, so it's something to keep in mind when choosing a school.

Determining Your Education Plan

There are many options, as mentioned, when it comes to pursing an education in the social work field. These include two-year community colleges, four-year colleges, and master's and PhD programs. This section will focus on undergraduate, or bachelor's, programs that can help you prepare for your career as a social worker.

It's a good idea to select roughly five to ten schools in a realistic location (for you) that offer the degree you want to earn. If you are considering online programs, include these in your list.

> **Tip:** Consider attending a university in your resident state (where you live and pay taxes) if possible, which will save you lots of money if you attend a state school. Private institutions don't typically discount resident student tuition costs.

HOW TO HAVE A GAP YEAR DURING (OR JUST FOLLOWING) A PANDEMIC

Although an earlier section in this chapter explored options for spending a gap year that would certainly offer invaluable experience to an aspiring social worker, unfortunately currently they are not all viable options due to the coronavirus—but that does not mean there aren't enriching activities and pursuits you can engage in to make a gap year just as worthwhile.

NextAdvisor offers some tips on how to make the most of a gap year, even if it is not possible to participate in a structured program such as the Peace Corps.[2] While they may not seem as exciting as traveling abroad, the point of a gap year is to help you refine your interests and gain additional skills before committing yourself to a college program. Here are some options to consider:

- **Learn a new skill.** Learn a new language. Become an expert in building an online platform if you want to grow your own private practice or reach a broader audience in the future online. Take a photography course. It's a good time to really develop yourself in new areas that may directly or indirectly affect you as a social worker, in that it can help you to look at the world and people differently.
- **Read.** Science has shown that reading fiction makes us more empathetic, which is a key skill for any social worker (or human, for that matter) to improve.[3]
- **Get a job to save money for college.** The virus has also hit many hard financially, so taking a year to earn money before heading off to school is certainly a valuable use of your time.
- **Volunteer.** There are virtual volunteer programs (check out VolunteerMatch) or you can do more local volunteering, such as buying groceries for an elderly neighbor.
- **Seek out remote internships.** Most people are currently working at home, and there are opportunities for interns to do the same.
- **Take online classes** at a local community college in a related subject.

Be sure you research the basic GPA and SAT or ACT requirements of each school as well. Although some community colleges do not require standardized tests for the application process, others do.

> **Note:** If you are planning to apply to a college or program that requires the ACT or SAT, advisors recommend that students take both the ACT and the SAT during their junior year of high school (spring at the latest). You can retake these tests and use your highest score, so be sure to leave time to retake early senior year if needed. You want your best score to be available to all the schools you're applying to by January of your senior year, which will also enable them to be considered with any scholarship applications. Keep in mind these are general timelines—be sure to check the exact deadlines and calendars of the schools to which you're applying!

SAT IS OPTIONAL—SHOULD I TAKE IT ANYWAY?

One of the consequences of the coronavirus pandemic related to education is that many universities changed aspects of their application processes. More than half of four-year colleges and universities in the United States—a staggering percentage—decided to make entrance exams like the SAT and ACT optional in 2021, and this is a change that may sustain for a lot longer.[4]

What exactly does "test optional" mean? It varies from school to school. Be sure you know what it means for any school you are considering applying to.

- Truly test optional means you decide if you want to submit your test scores. If you do, the scores will be taken into consideration along with other parts of the application. This implies that the test scores may carry less weight when compared with the other application elements but will be considered.
- Test-flexible schools will allow you to submit scores for the SAT or ACT or a different test in their place (such as an SAT Subject Test or AP test).
- Test-blind schools will not consider any scores, even if you include them in the application.

If you feel confident that your scores will be an asset to your application, then by all means take the test and submit the score. It will not hurt your chances and can only help them. And if you take the test and are not satisfied that the results will give your application a positive edge, then you are not obligated to submit the scores. So you really can't lose by preparing for and taking the tests.

Once you have found five to ten schools in a realistic location for you that offer the degree you want, spend some time on their websites studying the requirements for admissions. Important factors weighing on your decision of what schools to apply to should include whether you meet the requirements, your chances of getting in (but aim high!), tuition costs and availability of scholarships and grants, location, and the school's reputation and licensure/graduation rates.

> **Note:** Most colleges and universities will list the average stats for the last class accepted to the program, which will give you a sense of your chances of acceptance.

The order of these characteristics will depend on your grades and test scores, financial resources, work experience, and other personal factors. Taking everything into account, you should be able to narrow your list down to the institutes or schools that best match your educational or professional goals as well as your resources and other factors such as location and duration of study.

Schools to Consider When Pursuing a Career as a Social Worker

Some schools and programs have stronger reputations than others. Although you can certainly have a successful and satisfying career and experience without going to the "number-one" school in your field of study, it is a good idea to shop around, to compare different schools and get a sense of what they offer and what features of each are the most important—or least—to you.

Keep in mind that what is "great" for one person may not be as great for someone else. What might be a perfect school for you might be too difficult, too expensive, or not rigorous enough for someone else. Keep in mind the advice of the previous sections when deciding what you really need in a school.

As mentioned previously, you have a choice of degree type you want to pursue in order to become qualified as a social worker. This section will point you to the best programs for associate's, bachelor's, and master's degree programs.

GREAT SCHOOLS FOR SOCIAL WORK: CERTIFICATE AND ASSOCIATE'S DEGREE PROGRAMS

The following lists the top social work associate's degree programs as ranked in 2021 by Niche.com:[5]

- Cochise College, Sierra Vista, AZ
- Hutchinson Community College, Hutchinson, KS
- Casper College, Casper, WY
- Mercyhurst College, Erie, PA
- Las Positas College, Livermore, CA
- Santa Rosa Junior College, Santa Rosa, CA
- Harper College, Palatine, IL
- Northeastern Junior College, Sterling, CO
- Fox Valley Technical College, Appleton, WI
- Southern Arkansas University Tech, Camden, AR
- Northern Oklahoma College, Tonkawa, OK

Note: Keep in mind that although graduates holding an associate's of social work degree can explore a variety of entry-level work opportunities in the field, the degree does not qualify its holder to become a licensed social worker. It can, however, be a very good option for learning more about the field of social work and to help you in deciding if you want to continue your education and pursue a bachelor's degree at a later time.

> "The best part of my job is seeing change. While some cases are hard, social work is all about change. I enjoy seeing families better themselves and end a case with me in a better situation." —Katherine Barber, social worker

GREAT SCHOOLS FOR SOCIAL WORK: BACHELOR'S DEGREE PROGRAMS

This list of the best schools offering undergraduate programs in social work has been compiled by *U.S. News & World Report*:[6]

- University of Michigan, Ann Arbor, MI
- Washington University in St. Louis, St. Louis, MO

- Columbia University, New York, NY
- University of California, Berkeley, Berkeley, CA
- University of Chicago, Chicago, IL
- University of North Carolina, Chapel Hill, NC
- University of Washington, Seattle, WA
- University of Texas, Austin, Austin, TX
- Case Western Reserve University, Cleveland, OH
- Boston College, Chestnut Hill, MA
- Boston University, Boston, MA

GREAT SCHOOLS FOR SOCIAL WORK: MASTER'S DEGREE PROGRAMS

Although there are on-campus master's programs in social work, many people who already hold a bachelor's degree and are thinking about earning a master's choose to do so while they are working. Many of the best master's programs are available to follow online, which means you don't have to relocate and you can continue working while earning your degree if you choose.

> **Note:** If you want to pursue a career as a clinical social worker, keep in mind you will be required to hold a master's degree.

You can often earn your degree part-time to make this possible. Here are the top-ten schools offering such master's programs, according to College Choice.net:[7]

- University of California, Los Angeles, Los Angeles, CA
- Washington University in St. Louis, St. Louis, MO
- University of Maryland, Baltimore, Baltimore, MD
- University of North Carolina, Chapel Hill, NC
- University of Pennsylvania, Philadelphia, PA
- University of Washington, Seattle, WA
- University of California, Berkeley, Berkeley, CA
- University of Texas, Austin, Austin, TX
- University of Illinois, Urbana-Champaign, Champaign, IL
- University of Southern California, Los Angeles, CA

What's It Going to Cost You?

So the bottom line—what will your education end up costing you? First, some good news: According to *U.S. News & World Report*, the average tuition costs for colleges fell in 2020, which went against the standard trend of cost going up each year. For private colleges, costs fell by about 5 percent; for in-state colleges, the costs fell by 4 percent; and costs of out-of-state colleges (tuition for a person attending a state school but not in their resident state) have fallen by 6 percent.[8]

This trend appears to be continuing, according to an update by *U.S. News & World Report* that looks at tuition rates for the 2021–2022 school year.[9] This comes amid some calls for a tuition discount, as the COVID-19 pandemic has forced so many institutions to move to online course delivery.

Also according to *U.S. News & World Report*, the cost of an out-of-state school compared with an in-state school is 72 percent higher, so looking for a school in the state in which you reside is definitely a way to cut down the costs of your education.[10]

In addition, there are several financial aid options to help you find the funding to earn the degree you want. We cover those next.

School can be an expensive investment, but there are many ways to seek help paying for your education. *Hispanolistic/E+/Getty Images.*

> **WRITING A GREAT PERSONAL STATEMENT FOR ADMISSION**
>
> The personal statement you include with your application to college is extremely important, especially when your GPA and SAT/ACT scores are on the border of what is typically accepted. Write something that is thoughtful and conveys your understanding of the profession you are interested in, as well as your desire to practice in this field. Why are you uniquely qualified? Why are you a good fit for this university? These essays should be highly personal (the "personal" in personal statement). Will the admissions professionals who read it, along with hundreds of others, come away with a snapshot of who you really are and what you are passionate about?
>
> Look online for some examples of good ones, which will give you a feel for what works. Be sure to check your specific school for length guidelines, format requirements, and any other guidelines they expect you to follow.
>
> And of course, be sure to proofread it several times and ask a professional (such as your school writing center or your local library services) to proofread it as well.

Financial Aid: Finding Money for Education

Finding the money to attend college can seem out of reach. But you can do it if you have a plan before you actually start applying to college. If you get into your top-choice university, don't let the sticker cost turn you away. Financial aid can come from many different sources, and it's available to cover all different kinds of costs you'll encounter during your years in college, including tuition, fees, books, housing, and food.

The good news is that universities more often offer incentives or tuition discount aid to encourage students to attend. The market is often more competitive in the favor of the student, and colleges and universities are responding by offering more generous aid packages to a wider range of students than they used to. Here are some basic tips and pointers about the financial aid process:

- You apply for financial aid during your senior year. You must fill out the FAFSA (Free Application for Federal Student Aid) form at studentaid.gov, which can be filed starting October 1 of your senior year until June of the year you graduate. Because the amount of available aid is limited, it's best to apply as soon as you possibly can. See fafsa.gov to get started.

- Be sure to compare and contrast deals you get at different schools. There is room to negotiate with universities. The first offer for aid may not be the best you'll get.
- Wait until you receive all offers from your top schools and then use this information to negotiate with your top choice to see if they will match or beat the best aid package you received.
- To be eligible to keep and maintain your financial aid package, you must meet certain grade/GPA requirements. Be sure you are very clear on these academic expectations and keep up with them.
- You must reapply for federal aid every year.

> **Note:** Watch out for scholarship scams! You should never be asked to pay to submit the FAFSA form ("free" is in its name) or be required to pay a lot to find appropriate aid and scholarships. These are free services. If an organization promises you you'll get aid or that you have to "act now or miss out," these are both warning signs of a less reputable organization.
>
> Also, be careful with your personal information to avoid identity theft as well. Simple things like exiting your browser after visiting sites where you entered personal information go a long way. Don't share your student aid ID number with anyone either.

It's important to understand the different forms of financial aid that are available to you. That way, you'll know how to apply for different kinds and get the best financial aid package that fits your needs and strengths. The two main categories of financial aid are gift aid, which doesn't have to be repaid, and self-help aid, which is either loans that must be repaid or work-study funds that are earned. The next sections cover the various types of financial aid that fit in one of these areas.

GRANTS

Grants typically are awarded to students who have financial needs but can also be used in the areas of athletics, academics, demographics, veteran support, and special talents. They do not have to be paid back. Grants can come from federal agencies, state agencies, specific universities, and private organizations. Most federal and state grants are based on financial need.

Examples of grants are the Pell Grant, SMART Grant, and the Federal Supplemental Educational Opportunity Grant (FSEOG). Visit the US Department of Education's Federal Student Aid site for lots of current information about grants (see https://studentaid.ed.gov/types/grants-scholarships).

SCHOLARSHIPS

Scholarships are merit-based aid that does not have to be paid back. They are typically awarded based on academic excellence or some other special talent, such as music or art. Scholarships also fall under the areas of athletic-based, minority-based, aid for women, and so forth. These are typically not awarded by federal or state governments but instead come from the specific university you applied to as well as private and nonprofit organizations.

Be sure to reach out directly to the financial aid officers of the schools you want to attend. These people are great contacts that can lead you to many more sources of scholarships and financial aid. Visit http://www.gocollege.com/financial-aid/scholarships/types/ for lots more information about how scholarships in general work.

LOANS

Many types of loans are available especially to students to pay for their postsecondary education. However, the important thing to remember here is that loans must be paid back, with interest. Be sure you understand the interest rate you will be charged. This is the extra cost of borrowing the money and is usually a percentage of the amount you borrow. Is this fixed or will it change over time? Is the loan and interest deferred until you graduate (meaning you don't have to begin paying it off until after you graduate)? Is the loan subsidized (meaning the federal government pays the interest until you graduate)? These are all points you need to be clear about before you sign on the dotted line.

There are many types of loans offered to students, including need-based loans, non-need-based loans, state loans, and private loans. Two very reputable federal loans are the Perkins Loan and the Direct Stafford Loan. For more information about student loans, start at https://bigfuture.collegeboard.org/pay-for-college/loans/types-of-college-loans.

FEDERAL WORK-STUDY

The US federal work-study program provides part-time jobs for undergraduate and graduate students with financial need so they can earn money to pay for educational expenses. The focus of such work is on community service work and work related to a student's course of study. Not all colleges and universities participate in this program, so be sure to check with the school financial aid office if this is something you are counting on. The sooner you apply, the more likely you will get the job you desire and be able to benefit from the program, as funds are limited. See https://studentaid.ed.gov/sa/types/work-study for more information about this opportunity.

MEANINGFUL CONNECTIONS

Joy Koczka. *Courtesy of Joy Koczka.*

Joy Koczka, RSW, MSW, BSW, BA, is a mental health therapist who has worked with individuals struggling with substance use issues for several years. Joy began her career as a social worker and then obtained a master's degree in clinical social work in 2012. Since that time, Joy has been a therapist working in various capacities with both youth and adults. Joy specialized in dialectical behavior therapy (DBT) in her master's program whereby she developed a manual for delivering DBT with youth as well as a youth workbook. Joy has trained colleagues in the DBT approach as well as in trauma and attachment. Throughout Joy's career, she has worked with many individuals struggling with substance use. Joy is currently a therapist at Quest Health Inc., where she facilitates DBT group therapy and individual therapy with Indigenous populations, many of which struggle with substance abuse.

How is substance abuse counseling part of your role as a therapist?

As a therapist working within the mental health field, you often find that these individuals also struggle with substance use problems. The use of substances is often part of an individual's attempt to cope with the emotional issues whether it be anxiety, depression, PTSD, or any mental health issue. Unfortunately, the continued use of substances oftentimes becomes an addiction. As a therapist, I see addiction as a disease but also view it as a symptom of a deeper emotional problem. In my work, I have found that many people who struggle with addiction issues have experienced trauma in their life. I think it is essential that in order to help a client create meaningful change in their lives, we must address the underlying emotional issues they are struggling with. I believe that no matter what stage that individual is in in terms of their substance use, they deserve to be treated with dignity and respect. We need to start with "where the client is at," whether or not they are ready to address their substance use issues. I think professionals working with individuals with substance use issues need to consider the merit of "harm reduction" strategies, not only "abstinence" from substances.

Can you describe your educational background and career path to date?

I started off my career with a BSW and worked as a medical social worker and CFS worker. While obtaining my master's degree in clinical social work, I worked as a crisis clinician for youth mobile crisis in Winnipeg. Upon obtaining my MSW, I worked as a therapist for several years at Knowles Centre, which is a treatment center for youth with substantial emotional and behavioral issues, as well as a therapist for MacDonald Youth Services working with even more pronounced emotional and behavioral issues in youth. During this time, I also facilitated DBT group therapy with these youth. From there I went on to develop my own private practice and worked as a therapist for Blue Cross. I am currently a therapist for Quest Health Inc., where I facilitate DBT group therapy and provide individual therapy with Indigenous people. Throughout my whole career, I have worked with individuals struggling with substance use issues.

What is a typical day on the job for you?

My job is twofold: I spend two weeks of the month (Monday to Friday) facilitating DBT group therapy with Indigenous people, many of whom struggle with substance use issues. The other two weeks I travel to Indigenous communities and provide individual therapy.

What's the best or most satisfying part of your job?

I would say one of the most satisfying parts of my job is when I know I have made a meaningful connection with my client. I think developing a trusting relationship with your client is integral to helping them; without that you will not get anywhere in terms of helping them. The other satisfying part is when they thank me for the help I have given to them and when I believe that I have made a difference in their lives.

What's the most challenging part or stressful part of your job?

I think the most challenging part of my job is working against the systemic oppressive structures that exist for Indigenous people. My clients have experienced so much oppression in their lives stemming from the colonization of Indigenous people. As a result, these individuals have experienced intergenerational trauma. Something that did not need to happen happened and has caused so much damage to these individuals and is responsible for the many struggles they have today.

What has been the most surprising thing about your job as a therapist working with individuals who have substance abuse issues?

I would say the most surprising thing is the resilience that my clients have. I try as a therapist to "put myself in their shoes," and I am forever struck by their strength and willingness to keep trying.

What kinds of qualities do you consider advantageous to doing your job successfully?

There are many qualities that are essential to doing this type of work successfully. Not thinking of yourself as the "expert" in your client's lives is essential. They are the "experts" in their own lives, and it is important that therapy is done in a way that promotes an equal relationship between the therapist and client. Being nonjudgmental is also an essential quality. Being able to self-reflect and take a good look at yourself is integral and recognizing your own biases and challenging them because we all have them, and if we do not do this, it will have a negative effect on our work. Never thinking you know everything and having an open mind to new ideas and perspectives is essential. I am constantly learning and trying to improve my skills as a therapist, and I learn from my clients all the time.

How do you combat burnout?

Combatting burnout is something you need to do all the time. How I do this is by putting things into perspective. What we do is hard and we are working with individuals who have it the hardest, so it helps me to remember that there are people out there who are not struggling as badly. Having balance is extremely important. There is more to life than your job, so we need to remember that and try to have a life outside of work and know our limits. Self-care is important, and that could mean different things for different people. For me I know I am not taking care of myself when I am not sleeping enough, not eating as healthy as I should, and not taking the time to enjoy the company of friends and family. Being able to debrief with a colleague who does the same work you do is important. Using debriefing as a way to validate your own challenges and feelings as well as consulting regarding your work can go a long way to combat burnout.

How do you see your career or the substance abuse field evolving in the future?
I think the substance abuse field is currently evolving. The "harm reduction" approach to substance abuse is an evolving field. This means recognizing that abstinence from substances may not be possible for some people given the stage of change that they are in with their struggle against substances. Programs such as "managed alcohol programs" are but one example whereby individuals can slowly cut down on their substance use and not suffer from severe withdrawal. We must also recognize that "conventional treatment programs" do not always work for some people and that there are many ways to recover. Cultural healing practices are one of these examples. Some people can recover and heal from substance abuse on their own and do not require the help of a substance abuse counselor, so recognize that treatment or counseling is not always the answer for some people.

Summary

This chapter covered all the aspects of college and postsecondary schooling that you'll want to consider as you move forward. Remember that finding the right fit is especially important, as it increases the chances that you'll stay in school and earn your degree, as well as have an amazing experience while you're at it.

In this chapter, we discussed how to evaluate and compare your options in order to get the best education for the best deal. You also learned a little about scholarships and financial aid, how the SAT and ACT work if applicable, and how to write a unique personal statement that eloquently expresses your passions.

Use this chapter as a jumping-off point to dig deeper into your particular area of interest. Some tidbits of wisdom to leave you with:

- Take the SAT and ACT early in your junior year so you have time to take them again. Most universities automatically accept the highest scores while some schools do not require these test scores at all.
- Make sure that the institution you plan to attend has an accredited program in your field of study. Some professions follow national accreditation policies, while others are state-mandated and therefore differ across state lines. Do your research and understand the differences.

- Don't underestimate how important campus visits are, especially in the pursuit of finding the right academic fit. Come prepared to ask questions not addressed on the school website or in the literature.
- Your personal statement is a very important piece of your application that can set you apart from others. Take the time and energy needed to make it unique and compelling.
- Don't assume you can't afford a school based on the "sticker price." Many schools offer great scholarships and aid to qualified students. It doesn't hurt to apply. This advice especially applies to minorities, veterans, and students with disabilities.
- Don't lose sight of the fact that it's important to pursue a career that you enjoy, are good at, and are passionate about! You'll be a happier person if you don't.

At this point, your career goals and aspirations should be gelling. At the least, you should have a plan for finding out more information. Remember to do the research about the university, school, or degree program before you reach out and especially before you visit. Faculty and staff find students who ask challenging questions much more impressive than those who ask questions that can be answered by spending ten minutes on the school website.

In chapter 4, we go into detail about the next steps: writing a résumé and cover letter, interviewing well, follow-up communications, and more. This is information you can use to secure internships, volunteer positions, summer jobs, and more. It's not just for college grads. In fact, the sooner you can hone these communication skills, the better off you'll be in the professional world.

4

Writing Your Résumé and Interviewing

With each chapter of this book, we have narrowed the process of planning your social work career path, from the broadest of strokes—what social workers actually do—to how to plan your strategy and educational approach to making your dream job a reality.

In this chapter, we will cover the steps involved in applying for jobs or schools: how to prepare an effective, engaging, and informative résumé and slam-dunk an interview.

> **Note:** When you are applying for a job, how you present yourself in person and in writing will be a major determinant in your success and should receive just as much attention as the credentials you earn and the skills you hone.

Your résumé is your opportunity to summarize your experience, training, education, and goals and attract employers or school administrators. You can think of it like this: the goal of the résumé is to land the interview, and the goal of the interview is to land the job. Even if you do not have much working experience, you can still put together a résumé that expresses your interests and goals and the activities that illustrate your competence and interest.

As well as a résumé, you will be expected to write a cover letter that is basically your opportunity to reveal a little bit more about your passion and your motivation for a particular job or educational opportunity and often to express more about yourself personally to give a potential employer a sense of who you are and what drives you. And particularly because you are striving for a career in a field that relies on interpersonal interaction and on personal characteristics as well as earned credentials, it's wise to ensure your uniqueness, motivation, and commitment for working toward a meaningful cause—whatever your goal—comes through.

Giving the right impression is undoubtedly important, but don't let that make you nervous. In a résumé, cover letter, or interview, you want to put forward your best but genuine self. Dress professionally and proofread carefully (spelling, grammar, and typographical errors will be noticed and will work against you!), but ensure you are being yourself.

In this chapter, we will cover all of these important aspects of the job-hunting process, and by the end, you will feel confident and ready to present yourself as a candidate for the job you really want.

Writing Your Résumé

Writing your first résumé can feel very challenging because you have likely not yet gained a lot of experience in a professional setting. But don't fret: employers understand that you are new to the workforce or to the particular career you are seeking.

> **Note:** The right approach is never to exaggerate or invent experience or accomplishments but to present yourself as someone with a good work ethic and a genuine interest in the particular job or organization and use what you can to present yourself authentically and honestly.

There are some standard elements to an effective résumé that you should be sure to include. At the top should be your name, of course, as well as your e-mail address or other contact information. Always list your experience in chronological order, beginning with your current or most recent position—or whatever experience you want to share.

If you are a recent graduate with little work experience, you might want to begin with your education. If you've been in the working world for a while, you can opt to list your education or any certification you have at the end. List anywhere you have been published and any published work you may have edited.

> **Note:** You may need to customize your résumé for different purposes to ensure you are not filling it with information that does not directly link to your qualifications for a particular job.

If this is your first résumé, be sure you highlight your education where you can—any courses you've taken be it in high school or through a community college or any other place that offers training related to your job target. Also highlight any hobbies or volunteer experience you have. But be concise: one page is usually appropriate, especially for your very first résumé.

> **Tip:** Before preparing your résumé, try to connect with a hiring professional—a human resources person or hiring manager—in a similar position or organization you are interested in. They can give you advice on what employers look for and what information to highlight on your résumé, as well as what types of interview questions you can expect.

As important as your résumé's content is the way you design and format it. You can find many samples online of résumés that you can be inspired by. At TheBalanceCareers.com, for example, you can find many templates and design ideas.[1] You want your résumé to be attractive to the eye and formatted in a way that makes the key points easy to spot and digest—according to some research, employers take an average of six seconds to review a résumé, so you don't have a lot of time to get across your experience and value.

There is freedom and flexibility in how you organize the content of your résumé. The important thing is to present the most important and relevant information at the top. Your résumé needs to be easy to navigate and read.

WRITING AN OBJECTIVE

The objective section of your résumé is one of the most important, as it is the first section a recruiter or hiring manager will read and therefore where they will develop their first sense of you as a candidate. The objective should be brief but poignant. Definitely it should be focused and give a sense of you as a unique applicant. You don't want it to be generic or bland; show how creative you can be while keeping it professional. It's important to take your time and really refine your objective so you can stand out and attract employers or clients.

Be sure you do your research about the job and the organization to which you are applying. Know exactly what kind of social worker the organization is looking for. Then you can better craft your objective to highlight the ways in which you uniquely match their needs.

> **LINKING IN WITH IMPACT**
>
> As well as your paper or electronic résumé, creating a LinkedIn profile is a good way to highlight your experience and promote yourself, as well as to network. Joining professional organizations or connecting with other people in your desired field are good ways to keep abreast of changes and trends and work opportunities.
>
> The key elements of a LinkedIn profile are your photo, your headline, and your profile summary. These are the most revealing parts of the profile and the ones on which employers and connections will base their impression of you.
>
> The photo should be carefully chosen. Remember that LinkedIn is not Facebook or Instagram: it is not the place to share a photo of you acting too casually on vacation or at a party. According to Joshua Waldman, author of *Job Searching with Social Media for Dummies*, the choice of photo should be taken seriously and be done right.[2] His tips:
>
> - Choose a photo in which you have a nice smile.
> - Dress in professional clothing.
> - Ensure the background of the photo is pleasing to the eye. According to Waldman, some colors—like green and blue—convey a feeling of trust and stability.
> - Remember it's not a mug shot. You can be creative with the angle of your photo rather than stare directly into the camera.
> - Use your photo to convey some aspect of your personality.
> - Focus on your face. Remember that visitors to your profile will see only a small thumbnail image, so be sure your face takes up most of it.

Writing Your Cover Letter

As well as your résumé, most employers will ask that you submit a cover letter. This is a one-page letter in which you express your motivation, why you are interested in the organization or position, and what skills you possess that make you the right fit.

Here are some tips for writing an effective cover letter:

- As always, proofread your text carefully before submitting it.
- Be sure you have a letter that is focused on a specific job. Do not make it too general or one-size-fits-all. Your personality and uniqueness should

come through, or the recruiter or hiring manager will move on to the next application.
- Summarize why you are right for the position. Keep it relevant and specific to what the particular organization is looking for in a candidate and employee.
- Keep your letter to one page whenever possible.
- Introduce yourself in a way that makes the reader want to know more about you, and encourage them to review your résumé.
- Be specific about the job you are applying for. Mention the title and be sure it is correct.
- Try to find the name of the person who will receive your letter rather than keeping it nonspecific ("to whom it may concern").
- Be sure you include your contact details.
- End with a "call to action"—a request for an interview, for example.

Interviewing Skills

With your sparkling résumé, LinkedIn profile, and cover letter, you are bound to be called for an interview. This is an important stage to reach: you will have already gone through several filters—a potential employer has gotten a quick scan of your experience and has reviewed your LinkedIn profile and has made the decision to learn more about you in person.

There's no way to know ahead of time exactly what to expect in an interview, but there are many ways to prepare yourself. You can start by learning more about the person who will be interviewing you. In the same way recruiters and employers can learn about you online, you can do the same (for a business or a professional in a business—of course, you should not be digging up information on a private family!). You can see if you have any education or work experience in common or any contacts you both know. It's perfectly acceptable and even considered proactive in a positive way to research the person with whom you'll be interviewing, such as on LinkedIn.

Preparing yourself for the types of questions you will be asked to ensure you offer a thoughtful and meaningful response is vital to interview success. Particularly when you are applying for a job that will require and depend on how you present yourself conversationally, it is paramount that you respond in an effective, composed manner. Consider your answers carefully, and be prepared to support them with examples and anecdotes.

Be it in person or via video call, a job interview can be stressful. You can help calm your nerves and feel more confident if you prepare ahead by thinking about answers to questions you can anticipate being asked. *SDI Productions/E+/Getty Images.*

Here are some questions you should be prepared to be asked. It's a good idea to consider your answers carefully, without memorizing what you mean to say (as that can throw you off and will be obvious to the interviewer).

- Why did you decide to enter this field? What drives your passion for working in the social work profession?
- What is your educational background? What credentials did you earn?
- What experience do you have relating to social work?
- Are you a team player? Describe your usual role in a team-centered work environment. Do you easily assume a leadership role?

"I would say one of the most satisfying parts of my job is when I know I have made a meaningful connection with my client. I think developing a trusting relationship with your client is integral to helping them; without that you will not get anywhere in terms of helping them. The other satisfying part is when they thank me for the help I have given to them and when I believe that I have made a difference in their lives." —Joy Koczka, registered social worker and mental health specialist

BEWARE WHAT YOU SHARE ON SOCIAL MEDIA

Most of us engage in social media. Sites such as Facebook, Twitter, and Instagram provide us a platform for sharing photos and memories, opinions, and life events and reveal everything from our political stance to our sense of humor. It's a great way to connect with people around the world, but once you post something, it's accessible to anyone—including potential employers—unless you take mindful precaution.

Your posts may be public, which means you may be making the wrong impression without realizing it. More and more, people are using search engines like Google to get a sense of potential employers, colleagues, or employees, and the impression you make online can have a strong impact on how you are perceived. Approximately 70 percent of employers search for information on candidates on social media sites.[3]

Glassdoor.com offers the following tips for how to prevent your social media activity from sabotaging your career success:[4]

1. Check your privacy settings. Ensure that your photos and posts are only accessible to the friends or contacts you want to see them. You want to come across as professional and reliable.
2. Rather than avoid social media while searching for a job, use it to your advantage. It's to your advantage to have an online presence (as long as it's a flattering one). Give future employees a sense of your professional interest by "liking" pages or joining groups of professional organizations related to your career goals.
3. Grammar counts. Be attentive to the quality of writing of all your posts and comments.
4. Be consistent. With each social media outlet, there is a different focus and tone of what you are communicating. LinkedIn is very professional while Facebook is far more social and relaxed. It's okay to take a different tone on various social media sites, but be sure you aren't blatantly contradicting yourself.
5. Choose your username carefully. Remember, social media may be the first impression anyone has of you in the professional realm.

DRESSING APPROPRIATELY

How you dress for a job interview is very important to the impression you want to make. Remember that the interview, no matter what the actual environment in which you'd be working, is your chance to present your most professional self. Although you will not likely ever wear a suit to work, for the interview, it's the most professional choice.

> **Tip:** A suit is no longer an absolute requirement in many job interviews, but avoid looking too casual as it will give the impression you are not that interested.

WHAT EMPLOYERS EXPECT

Hiring managers and human resource professionals will also have certain expectations of you at an interview. The main thing is preparation: it cannot be overstated that you should arrive to an interview appropriately dressed, on time, unhurried, and ready to answer—and ask—questions.

For any job interview, demonstrate the main things employers will look for by doing the following:

- Have a thorough understanding of the organization and the job for which you are applying.
- Be prepared to answer questions about yourself and your relevant experience.
- Be poised and likeable but still professional. They will be looking for a sense of what it would be like to work with you on a daily basis and how your presence would fit in the culture of the business.
- Stay engaged. Listen carefully to what is being asked and offer thoughtful but concise answers. Don't blurt out answers you've memorized; really focus on what is being asked.
- Be prepared to ask your own questions. It shows how much you understand the flow of an organization or workplace and how you will contribute to it. Some questions you can ask:
    - What created the need to fill this position? Is it a new position or has someone left the organization?
    - Where does this position fit in the overall hierarchy of the organization?

- What are the key skills required to succeed in this job?
- What challenges might I expect to face within the first six months on the job?
- How does this position relate to the achievement of the organization's (or department's or boss's) goals?
- How would you describe the organization's culture?

You may find yourself interviewing virtually, using technology such as Zoom, rather than appearing in person. This is almost certainly the case during the time of the pandemic, but it may also be your circumstance if you are applying to a job far away from where you live.

To prepare for an online interview, you should follow the same preparation tips as you would for an in-person meeting, but be sure and test the technology ahead of time—including any application you need to use, passwords you require, microphone, camera, and so on. You can also test to see how your outfit or background appears to the person with whom you will be meeting. There is nothing worse than discovering your interviewer can't hear you properly or that there is anything unprofessional or inappropriate visible to the interviewer.

FALL IN LOVE WITH HELPING PEOPLE

Katherine Barber. *Courtesy of Katherine Barber.*

Katherine Barber has always been involved with serving the community and helping others. Once she started college, she fell in love with the profession of social work and helping others. Since college, Katherine has been working and volunteering in the child welfare system and has been with the Department of Children's Services for more than four years. Katherine has been able to help ensure child safety with many families in Tennessee and also help teach and train new social workers who are upcoming in the profession.

How did you choose social work as a career?

My parents were foster parents growing up, and even though I was their biological child, I fell in love with child welfare and the many foster siblings I had in my home. Once I started college, I learned about the social work degree and how hands-on the degree is with helping others and fell in love.

Can you describe your educational background and career path to date?

I graduated high school and completed my undergraduate at Middle Tennessee State University and got my bachelor's in social work. After working two years, I went back to school and obtained my master's in social work at the University of Tennessee, Knoxville.

What is a typical day on the job for you?

I work for the Department of Children's Services. A normal day for me is checking on families on my case load by checking on their services and completing monthly visits with them. I also investigate new referrals of possible child abuse and neglect, and some days are involved with meeting new families and having to investigate allegations against them.

What's the best or most satisfying part of your job?

The best part of my job is seeing change. While some cases are hard, social work is all about change. I enjoy seeing families better themselves and end a case with me in a better situation. There are cases where the change is me having to remove a child to ensure that they are safe. While that is hard, there is still healing in the process, and the end goal is for the family to begin on the journey of change.

What's the most challenging part or stressful part of your job?

Working with people and their lives is hard. People are unpredictable, and there are a lot of emotions involved with social work. The hardest part of this job is being supportive to families even when I may not want to support them due to their behaviors or actions toward me or others.

What has been the most surprising thing about your work in social work?

The most surprising thing I have learned with this job is the stories I have gained as a social worker. People will do crazy things and will tell you so many things that you never imagined if you just sit with them and listen to them without pushing an agenda on them.

What kinds of qualities and personal attributes do you consider advantageous to doing your job successfully?

People who are caring, empathic, and authentic are great in social work. The key to being a great social worker is having clear boundaries with yourself and your clients. Being a team player is very important in this line of work, and having a good and supportive group of people to work with is vital for this job to be manageable.

How do you combat burnout?

While everyone in the social work field will tell you self-care is the only way to handle the job, the more important lesson is knowing what type of self-care works well for you. I recommend having a good and clear understanding of yourself and learning what helps you as a person de-stress. I personally love hard-core workouts while my friends like yoga. Find what works for you and have not only "fun" self-care like eating at fun places and spending money but also healthy self-care that involves working your body, soul, and mind.

Summary

Congratulations on working through the book! You should now have a strong idea of your career goals within the social work field and how to realize them. In this chapter, we covered how to present yourself as the right candidate to a potential employer—and these strategies are also relevant if you are applying to a college or another form of training.

Here are some tips to sum it up:

- Your résumé should be concise and focused on only relevant aspects of your work experience or education. Although you can include some personal hobbies or details, they should be related to the job and your qualifications for it.
- Take your time with all your professional documents—your résumé, your cover letter, your LinkedIn profile—and be sure to proofread very carefully to avoid embarrassing and sloppy mistakes.
- Prepare yourself for an interview by anticipating the types of questions you will be asked and coming up with professional and meaningful responses.
- Equally, prepare some questions for you to ask your potential employer at the interview. This will show you have a good understanding and interest in the organization and what role you would have in it.

- Always follow up after an interview with a letter or an e-mail. An e-mail is the fastest way to express your gratitude for the interviewer's time and restate your interest in the position.
- Dress appropriately for an interview and pay extra attention to tidiness and hygiene.
- Be wary of what you share on social media sites while job searching. Most employers research candidates online, and what you have shared will influence their idea of who you are and what it would be like to work with you.

You've chosen to pursue a career in a competitive, challenging, but also broad and exciting field. We wish you great success in your future.

BEING OPEN TO THE PERSPECTIVES OF OTHERS

Christopher Collins. *Courtesy of Christopher Collins.*

Christopher Collins has had an interesting and varied career to date, including working as a book editor and launching a successful hot dog vendor business and of course working in social work. His interest lies in the policy, advocacy, and administrative areas of the field.

How did you choose social work as a career?

English had always been my best subject, and I enjoyed writing above everything else offered in school. It made sense that I would pursue journalism, which I did, and then I ended up in book publishing. Somewhere along the way, I realized that publishing was more or less a grind and, unless you were the author, left very little room for creativity.

I went to a career counselor and, after a series of tests, came away with the recommendation that I should pursue social work. I was surprised because I had little interest in being a traditional social worker; I couldn't see myself talking with clients day in and day out. The counselor continued to inform me on the myriad jobs available to someone pursuing social work, and many of them really made sense.

Can you describe your educational background and career path to date?

I have a bachelor's degree in journalism and a master's degree in social work. Right after undergraduate, I worked in a psychiatric group's office and began to think about the different areas associated with psychology. I then worked in publishing (in both the production and editorial ends), and then I went to graduate school.

In graduate school, I was among only about 10 percent who pursued a "macro" track, which was geared for those interested in the policy, advocacy, and administrative areas of social work. I worked for nonprofit organizations dedicated to civil rights, issues related specifically to youth development, and finally economic development.

What is a typical day on the job for you?

Because I don't see clients, most of my days resemble a typical office job. Working around advocacy usually means you will hold many meetings, usually working with other people and groups who share your goals and objectives. When you work in advocacy, it's likely you'll do a lot of writing and also develop trainings and other events related to your organization's goals.

What's the best or most satisfying part of your job?

While I don't get to see those "aha" moments some therapists experience, seeing policy makers seriously consider different perspectives can be very satisfying. And it is extremely satisfying to see real changes in public policy due to the efforts you and your team have put in.

What's the most challenging part or stressful part of your job?

Modern social work, whether working with one client or a group of stakeholders, is about being prepared, gathering consensus, and working on a deadline. You have to put away most notions of what "you" think is the best strategy and consider what is most effective for the other people in the room. While you are the content expert, the people you work with are ultimately the beneficiaries of the work. Making sure that work will get people where you need to be can be very challenging.

What has been the most surprising thing about your job as a social worker?

I am always surprised at the number of creative perspectives and practical opinions I get to hear every day. It is rare that you don't go home at the end of the day without having learned something you hadn't considered before.

What kinds of qualities and personal attributes do you consider advantageous to doing your job successfully?

One of the most important attributes of working in the field is being open to the perspectives of others. As I mentioned above, social work is very collaborative in nature. If you are the kind of person who can not only consider but value and champion the perspectives of people different from you, you will do well in this field.

How do you combat burnout?

Battling burnout is a common challenge in social work. Even though I don't work directly with people struggling with issues ranging from addictions to depression to serious mental illnesses, burnout still happens. Working every day around issues related to child abuse, for example, even on a policy level, can take a toll. People in other fields can sometimes have the luxury of not taking all their allotted vacation days. In social work, make sure you take the time you need, and try to spread your efforts around all the areas you're tasked with.

How do you see your career or the social work field evolving in the future?

The recent pandemic has attuned everyone to the notion that there are aspects of social work that lend itself to technology in a number of ways. While working with people, with those struggling with mental health in all its forms, will be the foundation of what social work is, technology will affect how, when, and where that happens.

Notes

Introduction

1. *Merriam-Webster*, "Social work," https://www.merriam-webster.com/dictionary/social%20work (accessed April 6, 2021).

2. David Sparkman, "Drug Abuse on the Rise because of COVID-19," *EHS Today*, August 24, 2020, https://www.ehstoday.com/covid19/article/21139889/drug-abuse-on-the-rise-because-of-the-coronavirus (accessed April 2, 2021).

3. Bureau of Labor Statistics, "Social Workers," https://www.bls.gov/ooh/community-and-social-service/mobile/social-workers.htm (accessed April 2, 2021).

Chapter 1

1. Paul H. Stuart, "Social Work Profession: History," *Encyclopedia of Social Work*, https://oxfordre.com/socialwork/view/10.1093/acrefore/9780199975839.001.0001/acrefore-9780199975839-e-623#acrefore-9780199975839-e-623-div1-2864 (accessed April 6, 2021).

2. Bureau of Labor Statistics, "Social Workers," https://www.bls.gov/ooh/community-and-social-service/mobile/social-workers.htm (accessed April 2, 2021).

3. Social Work Guide, "The Highest Paying States for Social Workers," August 17, 2020, https://www.socialworkguide.org/salaries/highest-paying-states-for-social-workers/ (accessed April 21, 2021).

Chapter 2

1. L. I. Hitchcock and M. Sage, "Actions That White Social Work Educators Can Do Now for Racial Justice" [blog post], Teaching and Learning in Social Work Blog, August 17, 2020, https://laureliversonhitchcock.org/2020/08/16/actions-that-white-social-work-educators-can-do-now-for-racial-justice/ (accessed May 3, 2021).

2. Jane E. Shersher, "Self Care Tips for Social Workers," SocialWorkLicensure.org, https://socialworklicensure.org/articles/self-care-tips/ (accessed April 21, 2021).

Chapter 3

1. Steven R. Antonoff, "College Personality Quiz," *U.S. News & World Report*, July 31, 2018, https://www.usnews.com/education/best-colleges/right-school/choices/articles/college-personality-quiz (accessed May 21, 2021).

2. Alex Gailey, "Taking a Gap Year during Coronavirus? Here's How to Make the Most of It," NextAdvisor, September 29, 2020, https://time.com/nextadvisor/in-the-news/gap-year-coronavirus/ (accessed May 21, 2021).

3. Claudia Hammond, "Does Reading Fiction Make Us Better People?" BBC, June 3, 2019, https://www.bbc.com/future/article/20190523-does-reading-fiction-make-us-better-people (accessed March 2, 2021).

4. FairTest, "1,425+ Accredited, 4-Year Colleges & Universities with ACT/SAT-Optional Testing Policies for Fall, 2022 Admissions," last updated May 17, 2021, https://fairtest.org/university/optional (accessed May 21, 2021).

5. Niche.com, "Top Two-Year Colleges with Social Work in America," https://www.niche.com/colleges/search/top-associates-degrees-in-social-work/ (accessed May 21, 2021).

6. *U.S. News & World Report*, "Best Schools for Social Work," https://www.usnews.com/best-graduate-schools/top-health-schools/social-work-rankings (accessed May 21, 2021).

7. CollegeChoice.net, "Top 10 MSW Programs," https://www.collegechoice.net/rankings/masters-in-social-work/ (accessed May 22, 2021).

8. Farran Powell and Emma Kerr, "See the Average College Tuition in 2020–2021," *U.S. News & World Report*, September 14, 2020, https://www.usnews.com/education/best-colleges/paying-for-college/articles/paying-for-college-infographic (accessed May 2, 2021).

9. Emma Kerr, "How Colleges Are Adjusting Their 2021–2022 Tuition," *U.S. News & World Report*, January 21, 2021, https://www.usnews.com/education/best-colleges/paying-for-college/articles/how-colleges-are-adjusting-their-2021-2022-tuition (accessed May 2, 2021).

10. Powell and Kerr, "See the Average College Tuition."

Chapter 4

1. The Balance Careers, https://www.thebalancecareers.com/student-resume-examples-and-templates-2063555 (accessed May 21, 2021).

2. Joshua Waldman, *Job Searching with Social Media for Dummies* (Hoboken, NJ: John Wiley & Sons, 2013).

3. SecurityMagazine.com, "70 Percent of Employers Check Candidates' Social Media Profiles," September 23, 2018, www.securitymagazine.com/articles/89441-percent-of-employers-check-candidates-social-media-profiles (accessed May 21, 2021).

4. Alice A. M. Underwood, "9 Things to Avoid on Social Media while Looking for a New Job," January 3, 2018, https://www.glassdoor.com/blog/things-to-avoid-on-social-media-job-search/ (accessed October 30, 2020).

Glossary

bachelor's degree: A four-year degree awarded by a college or university.

behavioral science: The study of human or animal behavior.

burnout: Feeling of physical and emotional exhaustion caused by overworking.

campus: The location of a school, college, or university.

career assessment test: A test that asks questions particularly geared to identify skills and interests to help inform the test taker on what type of career would suit them.

clinical social workers: Social workers who focus on the assessment, diagnosis, treatment, and prevention of mental illness, emotional problems, and other behavioral disturbances.

colleagues: The people with whom you work.

community college: A two-year college that awards associate's degrees.

counselor: A qualified person who counsels or advises a person through a difficult problem.

cover letter: A document that usually accompanies a résumé and allows a candidate applying to a job or a school or internship an opportunity to describe their motivation and qualifications.

educational background: The degrees a person has earned and schools attended.

empathy: The quality of being able to understand the feelings of another person.

financial aid: Various means of receiving financial support for the purposes of attending school. This can be a grant or scholarship, for example.

gap year: A year between high school and higher education or employment during which a person can explore their passions and interests, often while traveling.

General Education Development (GED) degree: A degree that is the equivalent to a high school diploma and earned without graduating from high school.

industry: The people and activities involved in one type of business, such as the business of publishing.

in-state school: A public college that exists in the state in which you are a resident. In-state schools offer lower tuitions to state residents.

internship: A work experience opportunity that lasts for a set period of time and can be paid or unpaid.

interpersonal: Relating to the relationship between people.

interpersonal skills: The ability to communicate and interact with other people in an effective manner.

interviewing: A part of the job-seeking process in which a candidate meets with a potential employer, usually face-to-face, in order to discuss their work experience and education and seek information about the position.

job market: A market in which employers search for employees and employees search for jobs.

major: The subject or course of study in which you choose to earn your degree.

master's degree: A degree that is sought by those who have already earned a bachelor's degree in order to further their education.

mental health: A person's health regarding their psychological and emotional well-being.

networking: The processes of building, strengthening, and maintaining professional relationships as a way to further your career goals.

nonjudgmental behavior: The ability to observe and accept another without qualifying a behavior as "right" or "wrong."

out-of-state school: A public college that exists in a state other than the one in which you are a resident. These schools have higher tuitions for nonstate residents.

private practice: An independent business—for example, a social work service provider—that is not controlled or paid for by the government or a larger company.

psychology: The scientific study of the human mind and its functions.

résumé: A document, usually one page, that outlines a person's professional experience and education and is designed to give potential employers a sense of a candidate's qualifications.

social media: Websites and applications that enable users to create and share content online for networking and social-sharing purposes. Examples include Facebook and Instagram.

sociology: The study of the development, structure, and functioning of human society.

substance abuse: Long-term use or dependence on alcohol or drugs, including daily use, inability to reduce consumption, and negative impacts on social relationships, career, and other areas of function.

substance abuse social worker: A specific type of social worker who assesses and treats people and families of people who are suffering from substance abuse problems.

therapy: Treatment for a particular disorder. Therapy can be delivered medicinally or through "talk therapy" in groups or individually.

trauma: An experience that is deeply distressing physically or emotionally.

yuition: The money you have to pay for education, be it a university degree or a certification.

work culture: A concept that defines the beliefs, philosophy, thought processes, and attitudes of employees in a particular organization.

Further Resources

The following websites, magazines, and organizations can help you further investigate and educate yourself on social work–related topics, all of which will help you as you take the next steps in your career, now and throughout your professional life.

Publications and Websites

ONLINE MSW PROGRAMS

https://www.onlinemswprograms.com/careers/child-welfare-social-work/

A resource created to help potential students find and research online Master of Social Work (MSW) degree programs. It also provides perspectives from people working in the field about their jobs and their educational backgrounds.

SOCIAL WORK TODAY

https://www.socialworktoday.com/

A resource for social work professionals that provides in-depth content examining the difficult issues, challenges, and successes of social workers.

THE NEW SOCIAL WORKER

https://www.socialworker.com/magazine

A social work careers magazine for students or recent graduates of social work programs and those who wish to learn more about and grow in the field.

ADDICTION AND RECOVERY NEWS

https://addictionandrecoverynews.wordpress.com/

Focuses on the stigma, media coverage, and research surrounding drug and alcohol addiction.

PROFESSIONAL SOCIAL WORK

https://www.basw.co.uk/resources/professional-social-work-psw/digital-editions

A monthly magazine dedicated to social work professionals, providing news, analysis, feature articles, interviews, letters, and opinion pieces. Focused on UK social work but with content applicable to an international audience.

Organizations

NATIONAL ASSOCIATION OF SOCIAL WORKERS

https://www.socialworkers.org/

The largest membership organization of professional social workers in the world, NASW works to enhance the professional growth and development of its members, to create and maintain professional standards, and to advance sound social policies.

COUNCIL ON SOCIAL WORK EDUCATION

https://www.cswe.org/

An organization representing social work education in the United States. Its members include more than eight hundred accredited baccalaureate and master's degree social work programs, as well as individual social work educators, practitioners, and agencies dedicated to advancing quality social work education.

ASSOCIATION OF SOCIAL WORK BOARDS

https://www.aswb.org/

Provides support and services to the social work regulatory community to advance safe, competent, and ethical practices and to strengthen public protection. ASWB's goal is for all social workers to be licensed in order to protect clients and client systems.

Bibliography

Antonoff, Steven R. "College Personality Quiz." *U.S. News & World Report*, July 31, 2018. https://www.usnews.com/education/best-colleges/right-school/choices/articles/college-personality-quiz. Accessed May 21, 2021.

The Balance Careers. https://www.thebalancecareers.com/student-resume-examples-and-templates-2063555. Accessed May 21, 2021.

Bureau of Labor Statistics. "Social Workers." https://www.bls.gov/ooh/community-and-social-service/mobile/social-workers.htm. Accessed April 2, 2021.

Careers in Psychology. "Preparing for a Private Counseling Practice." https://careersinpsychology.org/how-prepare-private-counseling-practice/. Accessed February 17, 2021.

CollegeChoice.net. "Top 10 MSW Programs." https://www.collegechoice.net/rankings/masters-in-social-work/. Accessed May 22, 2021.

FairTest. "1,425+ Accredited, 4-Year Colleges & Universities with ACT/SAT-Optional Testing Policies for Fall, 2022 Admissions." Last updated May 17, 2021. https://fairtest.org/university/optional. Accessed May 21, 2021.

Gailey, Alex. "Taking a Gap Year during Coronavirus? Here's How to Make the Most of It." NextAdvisor, September 29, 2020. https://time.com/nextadvisor/in-the-news/gap-year-coronavirus/. Accessed May 21, 2021.

Hammond, Claudia. "Does Reading Fiction Make Us Better People?" BBC, June 3, 2019. https://www.bbc.com/future/article/20190523-does-reading-fiction-make-us-better-people. Accessed March 2, 2021.

Hitchcock, L. I., and M. Sage. "Actions That White Social Work Educators Can Do Now for Racial Justice" [blog post]. Teaching and Learning in Social Work Blog, August 17, 2020. https://laureliversonhitchcock.org/2020/08/16/actions-that-white-social-work-educators-can-do-now-for-racial-justice/. Accessed May 3, 2021.

Kerr, Emma. "How Colleges Are Adjusting Their 2021–2022 Tuition." *U.S. News & World Report*, January 21, 2021. https://www.usnews.com/education/best-colleges/paying-for-college/articles/how-colleges-are-adjusting-their-2021-2022-tuition. Accessed May 2, 2021.

LiveCareer.com. "Child Care Provider Resume Objective Example." https://www.livecareer.com/resume/objectives/child-care/provider. Accessed June 17, 2021.

Merriam-Webster. "Social work." https://www.merriam-webster.com/dictionary/social%20work. Accessed April 6, 2021.

Niche.com. "Top Two-Year Colleges with Social Work in America." https://www.niche.com/colleges/search/top-associates-degrees-in-social-work/. Accessed May 21, 2021.

Powell, Farran, and Emma Kerr. "See the Average College Tuition in 2020–2021." *U.S. News & World Report*, September 14, 2020. https://www.usnews.com/education/best-colleges/paying-for-college/articles/paying-for-college-infographic. Accessed May 2, 2021.

SecurityMagazine.com. "70 Percent of Employers Check Candidates' Social Media Profiles." September 23, 2018. www.securitymagazine.com/articles/89441-percent-of-employers-check-candidates-social-media-profiles. Accessed May 21, 2021.

Shersher, Jane E. "Self Care Tips for Social Workers." SocialWorkLicensure.org. https://socialworklicensure.org/articles/self-care-tips/. Accessed April 21, 2021.

Social Work Guide. "The Highest Paying States for Social Workers." August 17, 2020. https://www.socialworkguide.org/salaries/highest-paying-states-for-social-workers/. Accessed April 21, 2021.

Sparkman, David. "Drug Abuse on the Rise because of COVID-19." *EHS Today*, August 24, 2020. https://www.ehstoday.com/covid19/article/21139889/drug-abuse-on-the-rise-because-of-the-coronavirus. Accessed April 1, 2021.

Stuart, Paul H. "Social Work Profession: History." *Encyclopedia of Social Work*. https://oxfordre.com/socialwork/view/10.1093/acrefore/9780199975839.001.0001/acrefore-9780199975839-e-623#acrefore-9780199975839-e-623-div1-2864. Accessed April 6, 2021.

Underwood, Alice A. M. "9 Things to Avoid on Social Media while Looking for a New Job." Glassdoor, January 3, 2018. https://www.glassdoor.com/blog/things-to-avoid-on-social-media-job-search/. Accessed October 30, 2020.

U.S. News & World Report. "Best Schools for Social Work." https://www.usnews.com/best-graduate-schools/top-health-schools/social-work-rankings. Accessed May 21, 2021.

Waldman, Joshua. *Job Searching with Social Media for Dummies*. Hoboken, NJ: John Wiley & Sons, 2013.

About the Author

Tracy Brown Hamilton is a writer, editor, and journalist based in the Netherlands. She has written several books on topics ranging from careers to media, economics to pop culture. She lives with her husband and three children.